P9-DUP-554

The Business Of Listening

A Practical Guide to Effective Listening

Third Edition

Diana Bonet

A Fifty-Minute™ Series Book

This Fifty-Minute™ book is designed to be "read with a pencil." It is an excellent workbook for self-study as well as classroom learning. All material is copyright-protected and cannot be duplicated without permission from the publisher. *Therefore, be sure to order a copy for every training participant by contacting:*

1-800-442-7477

CrispLearning.com

The Business of Listening

A Practical Guide to Effective Listening

Third Edition

Diana Bonet

CREDITS:
Senior Editor: **Debbie Woodbury**
Production Editor: **Jill Zayszly**
Production Manager: **Judy Petry**
Design: **Amy Shayne**
Production Artist: **Zach Hooker**
Cartoonist: **Ralph Mapson**

All rights reserved. No part of this book may be reproduced or transmitted in any form or by any means now known or to be invented, electronic or mechanical, including photocopying, recording, or by any information storage or retrieval system without written permission from the author or publisher, except for the brief inclusion of quotations in a review.

© 1988, 1994, 2001 Crisp Publications, Inc.
Printed in the United States of America by Von Hoffmann Graphics, Inc.

CrispLearning.com

01 02 03 04 10 9 8 7 6 5 4 3 2 1

Library of Congress Catalog Card Number 00-111457
Bonet, Diana
The Business of Listening
ISBN 1-56052-590-8

Learning Objectives For:

THE BUSINESS OF LISTENING

The objectives for *The Business of Listening* are listed below. They have been developed to guide you, the reader, to the core issues covered in this book.

The objectives of this book are:

- ❑ 1) To explain the how and why of active listening
- ❑ 2) To show the results of good listening
- ❑ 3) To direct the improvement of listening skills

Assessing Your Progress

In addition to the learning objectives, Crisp Learning has developed an **assessment** that covers the fundamental information presented in this book. A 25-item, multiple-choice and true-false questionnaire allows the reader to evaluate his or her comprehension of the subject matter. To learn how to obtain a copy of this assessment please call: **1-800-442-7477** and ask to speak with a Customer Service Representative.

Assessments should not be used in any employee selection process.

About the Author

Diana Bonet has devoted her 20-year career to developing and conducting seminars in business writing, technical writing, and listening skills. Ms. Bonet was one of the first 100 members of the International Listening Association when it began in the late 1970s. Her client list includes major corporations and government agencies throughout the United States, Canada, and Europe.

Presently Ms. Bonet lives with her husband in Northern California where she continues her work. She also acts as a writing coach for new writers and enjoys freelance editing assignments. In her spare time she is an avid gardener.

Other books by Ms. Bonet include *Clear Writing: A Step-by-Step Guide*, *Vocabulary Improvement*, and *Easy English: Basic Grammar & Usage.*

Dedication

This book is dedicated to my husband, Gary Romero, who has shown me that being a good listener is easier than living with one.

Preface

If you want to improve your ability to listen effectively in your business and personal life, this book is for you. Most of us are not good listeners. While at work, we normally listen at about 25% of our listening capacity. Most of us think we are good listeners, and that overconfidence may be the reason for our downfall. Even if we devote full concentration to listening, we cannot listen at 100% efficiency for very long. And at 100% efficiency, the message we are listening to must be urgent to sustain our attention.

Aside from breathing, humans listen more than anything. Carefully reading this book will help you learn to listen better on the job and at home. Before good listening can happen you must want to be a good listener. Whether you are an administrative assistant, an account executive, a programmer, or a project manager, you can improve your listening if you have the desire, the interest, a high level of concentration, self-discipline, and a positive attitude.

This book will provide you with important listening know-how. It is a self-study introduction to the basic skills you need to become a better listener. It provides many helpful suggestions for incorporating more effective listening skills into your business day. However, listening styles and motivation are highly individual, so there is no claim as to how much your listening skills will improve. We offer many suggestions for improvement, along with some motivation to help you make constructive changes in your listening style. After completing *The Business of Listening*, you can practice your newfound listening awareness on co-workers, family, and friends.

With the publication of this third edition of *The Business of Listening* an entire section has been added and devoted to the four types of Listening Styles. Understanding your own listening style, and that of others, will help you adjust your own behavior to improve your ability to listen and communicate with others.

Use *The Business of Listening* as a reference, and challenge yourself to practice until you have mastered each new skill. Remember: practice does not make perfect–it makes permanent. Listening well will help you function more effectively in both your business and personal life. So pick up your pencil, tune in, and turn to Part 1.

Happy Listening.

Diana Bonet

Diana Bonet

Contents

PART 5: Ten Tips for Tip-Top Listening

Summary

The Business of Listening

In Business…

Effective listening lays the foundation for *clear understanding.*

Clear understanding allows an *appropriate response.*

An appropriate response facilitates *high-quality communication.*

High-quality communication promotes *organizational cooperation.*

Organizational cooperation improves *employee morale.*

High morale increases *job commitment.*

Job commitment leads to *peak productivity.*

Listening is Good Business!

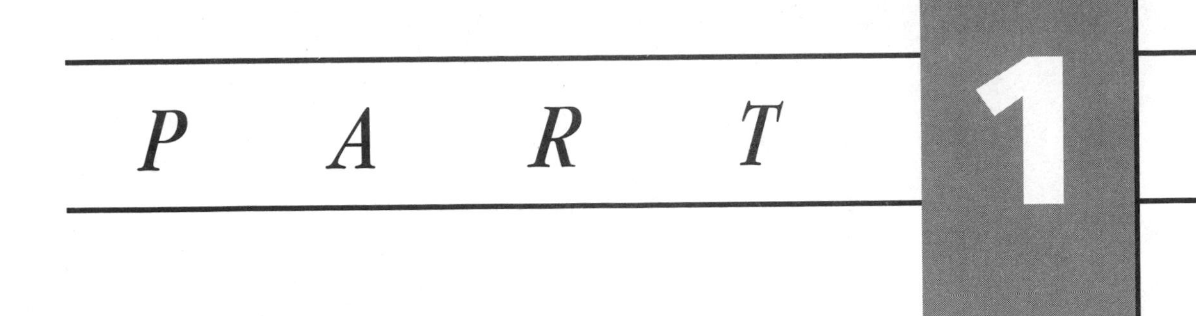

PART 1

Why Should You Listen?

What's in It for You?

At least half of all communication time is spent listening. Experts in a dozen studies have verified that we listen more than we perform any other activity, except breathing. Listening is the "receiving" part of communication. Listening is:

- ➤ Receiving information through your ears (and eyes)
- ➤ Giving meaning to that information
- ➤ Deciding what you think (or feel) about that information
- ➤ Responding to what you hear

Listening-related work activities

Much of our listening is work-related. We spend countless hours of our working lives involved in listening-related activities. Following is a partial list of work-related activities that involve listening. Put a check mark (✔) next to those that apply to you.

___ attending meetings, briefings, and lectures

___ personal counseling (one-on-one)

___ giving instructions

___ receiving instructions

___ interviewing others

___ making decisions based on verbal information

___ selling or marketing a product or service

___ managing others

___ helping clients

___ servicing other groups or departments

___ using the telephone

If you are like most people, you checked many of the activities on this list. What other work-related activities can you think of that involve listening?

____

____

____

____

What is the business of listening? More important, what's in it for you? Put a check mark (✔) next to those items with which you agree.

Listening effectively can:

- ❑ Increase your income
- ❑ Improve your company's profits
- ❑ Make you more promotable
- ❑ Increase your job satisfaction
- ❑ Improve your ability to solve problems
- ❑ Keep you aware of what is going on in your organization

The Benefits of Listening—A Quiz

Read each of the following statements. Write **T** for true or **F** for false next to each of the following questions about the benefits of good listening in business relationships. Check your answers with those of the author in the back of this book.

___ 1. Skill in listening improves your self-confidence.

___ 2. People like you when you listen to them.

___ 3. Good listeners are usually more efficient in completing their work.

___ 4. Careful listening helps to settle disagreements before they get bigger.

___ 5. Intelligent responses are easier when you listen.

___ 6. More decisions are made by "shooting from the hip" than by listening to the opinions of others.

___ 7. Learning to listen to clients helps you respond more quickly to their needs.

___ 8. Few good listeners are promoted to top management positions.

___ 9. Good listeners are not often embarrassed by unnecessary mistakes.

___ 10. Handling distractions is difficult for good listeners.

What's in It for Your Organization?

Successful organizations rely heavily upon listening as an important productivity tool. They seek to hire people who have good listening and communication skills. Employees who listen effectively help their employers by:

- Understanding problems
- Sustaining attention
- Retaining information
- Clarifying procedures
- Building relationships

Asleep at the Switch: The Cost of Lazy Listening

Most of us are not good listeners. We listen at about 25% of our potential, which means we ignore, forget, distort, or misunderstand 75% of what we hear. Hard to believe perhaps, but true. Such lazy listening habits can be very costly, both to our business and to ourselves.

Poor listening is a significant problem in business today because business relies on clear communication. When communication breaks down, costly mistakes occur. Organizations pay for these mistakes with lower profits, and consumers pay for the same mistakes with higher prices.

Lazy listening is a hidden cost of doing business. Suppose you were employed by a large international company with 10,000 employees. If each person in the company made one $100 error each year because of poor listening, the company would lose a million dollars. This loss would be especially bad news if your company had a profit-sharing plan or was forced to lay off workers because of poor earnings.

The following examples are true stories of the costs of lazy listening.

CASE STUDIES

A sales manager for a large company asked his accounting department how he could charge off a $100,000 error caused by a dispatcher who routed a fleet of drivers to deliver building material to the wrong state. The dispatcher heard the city (Portland) but not the state (Maine). The result was eight trucks 3,000 miles off course in Portland, Oregon. How could this problem have been avoided?

Three computer sales representatives from different companies presented their products to a historian who had special application needs. The historian was a dealer in rare manuscripts and explained to each sales representative what computer functions were required. Two of the sales representatives did not listen and presented products that were inappropriate. The third understood what the historian wanted, and she got the order. The manuscript dealer was impressed with only one thing, and it wasn't the hardware because he didn't know much about computers. He did know that two people didn't listen and the third one did. He bought his computer from the person who listened. What was the cost to the other two companies?

Linda recently cut short a business trip to attend an important investment dinner meeting with her husband. She hurried from the airport, dressed for dinner, and met her husband at the restaurant. An hour-and-a-half later their financial advisor had not arrived. A phone call revealed that they were at the right restaurant, but on the wrong night. The dinner was rescheduled, but Linda sacrificed profitable business she would have closed had she kept her original trip schedule. How can Linda avoid this problem in the future?

What Do You Know About Listening?

Write **T** for true or **F** for false next to each of the following questions about listening in order to check your present awareness of this important communication skill. See the author's comments in the back of this book.

___ 1. People who get the facts right are always good listeners.

___ 2. Listening involves more than your ears.

___ 3. Hearing is the same as listening.

___ 4. Good listening comes naturally when we pay attention.

___ 5. You can listen well and do other things at the same time.

___ 6. Posture affects listening.

___ 7. Most listening distractions can be controlled.

___ 8. If you can't remember something, you weren't really listening.

___ 9. Listening is a passive activity.

___ 10. Good listeners never interrupt.

Next, read "Fifty Good Reasons to Become a better Listener" on the following page. Circle those that are most important to you.

FIFTY GOOD REASONS TO BECOME A BETTER LISTENER

1. To learn something
2. To be entertained
3. To understand a situation
4. To get information
5. To be respectful
6. To be responsible
7. To prevent accidents
8. To be a team player
9. To ask intelligent questions
10. To improve confidence
11. To protect freedom
12. To find out people's needs
13. To negotiate effectively
14. To be valued and trusted
15. To use money wisely
16. To be more efficient and productive
17. To evaluate accurately
18. To make comparisons
19. To share in your children's lives
20. To analyze the speaker's purpose
21. To be liked by others
22. To get the best value
23. To improve self-discipline
24. To build relationships
25. To solve problems
26. To show compassion
27. To satisfy curiosity
28. To be safe
29. To be a good lover
30. To make intelligent decisions
31. To prevent waste
32. To make money
33. To avoid embarrassment
34. To stay out of trouble
35. To save time
36. To be an informed consumer
37. To be a supportive friend
38. To give an appropriate response
39. To enjoy the sounds of nature
40. To create "win-win" situations
41. To control distractions
42. To increase concentration
43. To improve your vocabulary
44. To stay healthy
45. To be prepared for shifts in a conversation
46. To be a better family member
47. To settle disagreements
48. To maintain a flexible attitude
49. To improve your personality
50. To use the gift of hearing

The Joy of Small Change

To improve the listening skills suggested in this book, we must be both motivated and educated. We must believe that each small change in lazy listening habits has value for us.

Change can be hard work. Setbacks occur just when we think we're making progress. To change our listening habits we must believe that the new skills we are gaining are worth more to us than the unproductive habits we are giving up. As you work to change your behavior and practice the listening techniques presented in the pages ahead, the following suggestions will be helpful. To change effectively, it is recommended that you:

1. **Notice small changes**. Recognize your improvements and give yourself a pat on the back as they occur. Acknowledging improvements is a form of positive reinforcement.

2. **Keep a card** in your pocket to note significant listening habit changes, such as:

   ➤ Paying attention in a boring meeting

   ➤ Receiving positive feedback from your manager about your communication skills

   ➤ Preventing yourself from interrupting a co-worker at coffee

3. **Acknowledge setbacks** but do not give in to them. Failure to learn from mistakes is the only real failure.

4. **Stay with it**. Unless you consciously work to improve your listening skills, you will find it easy to slip back into your old, bad habits.

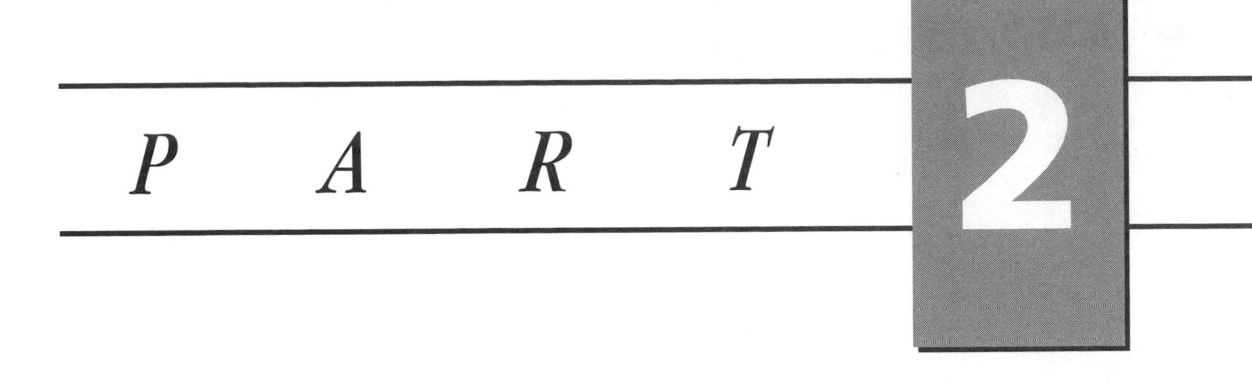

Four Key Elements of Good Listening

How to Be a Good Listener

Good listening is an active, integrated communication skill that demands energy and know-how. It is purposeful, powerful, and productive. To listen effectively we must hear and select information from the speaker, give it meaning, determine how we feel about it, and respond in a matter of seconds!

We must also understand the speaker's purpose to know how to listen most effectively. The speaker's purpose influences the way we listen and how we perceive what is said. The speaker and the listener must have the same purpose if communication is to be effective. Next time you listen to someonc, make sure you are aware of the speaker's purpose.

Is he or she:

- ❑ Entertaining you?
- ❑ Providing critical data?
- ❑ Persuading you?
- ❑ Sharing feelings?
- ❑ Making small talk?

For example, if Joe is making small talk, you can enjoy the conversation for its own sake. You and Joe are building rapport and strengthening your relationship with this casual conversation. However, if you are in a meeting with Joe, and he is informing you of important changes in inventory procedure, you will be listening for facts, numbers, and other key information. You will probably be taking notes, and you will ask questions to clarify what you do not understand.

Four Key Elements

The four key elements of the listening process describe what good listeners do to listen more effectively in any situation. These elements are:

1. Hear the message
2. Interpret the message
3. Evaluate the message
4. Respond to the message

ARE YOU A GOOD LISTENER?

Before reading the elements of good listening, consider what you already know about yourself as a listener. Remember that we listen differently at different times to different people. Evaluate yourself at the beginning of this section, then put a date on your calendar two weeks from today and evaluate again to see if any of your numbers change. They will change positively if you commit to doing something about negative listening habits. It's up to you.

Following are 10 characteristics of a good listener. On a scale of 1–5, with 5 being the highest, fill in the blanks to indicate the degree to which you already practice these positive listening behaviors. Go through the list twice, first rating yourself with the person you listen to the best, then rating yourself with the person to whom you find it most difficult to listen.

	Best	**Worst**	
1.	___	___	I make regular eye contact with the speaker.
2.	___	___	I ask questions for clarification.
3.	___	___	I show concern by acknowledging feelings.
4.	___	___	I restate or paraphrase some of the speaker's words to show that I understand.
5.	___	___	I seek first to understand, then to be understood.
6.	___	___	I am poised and emotionally controlled.
7.	___	___	I react non-verbally, with a smile, a nod, a frown, or a touch, if appropriate.
8.	___	___	I pay close attention and do not let my mind wander.
9.	___	___	I act responsibly on what I hear.
10.	___	___	I stick to the subject.

DO YOU HAVE BAD LISTENING HABITS?

Following is a list of 10 bad habits of listening. On a scale of 1–5, with 5 being the worst case, indicate the degree to which you are guilty of these poor listening habits. Rate yourself twice, first with the person you listen to the best, then with the person to whom you find it most difficult to listen. Be honest with yourself. Recognizing how you listen is the first step toward constructive change.

	Best	Worst	
1.	___	___	I interrupt often.
2.	___	___	I jump to conclusions.
3.	___	___	I finish other people's sentences.
4.	___	___	I change the subject without warning.
5.	___	___	I make up my mind before I have all of the information.
6.	___	___	I only half-way pay attention.
7.	___	___	I don't give any response.
8.	___	___	I am impatient.
9.	___	___	I become defensive right away.
10.	___	___	I think about my reply while the other person is speaking.

Key Element 1: Hear the Message

The brain recognizes sound as it enters the ear. Then, other "listening channels" such as our eyes and our feelings seek confirmation of the message from the speaker's non-verbal feedback, such as body language and tone of voice. Hearing is the beginning of the listening process. Hearing is non-selective and involuntary. However, when you choose to listen, it is on purpose.

Listening Is Voluntary

From the constant noise around us, we select what we want to listen to. This information moves from short term memory (STM) to long term memory (LTM). Short term memory is a "holding pen" for incoming signals from our five senses. In order to protect us from too much stimulation STM has a limited capacity and is easily disrupted. For instance, a mail clerk would not likely retain much information from a technical discussion about data transport protocols because he or she would have no use for the message. The information would probably be held in STM for 1 to 30 seconds and then dismissed. If the information we hear is not recognized and selected for processing, it is dismissed from STM and not remembered.

In a sense, we are preprogrammed. Our choices of what to listen to come from previous choices based on interests and needs. John enjoys investing in the stock market, so he always has his "ears open" for tips on hot stocks. Ellie "tunes in" whenever someone is discussing consumer rights. Julio "catches" the football scores each Sunday to track his favorite teams. In other words, we choose what we want to listen to, and often it is based on our past choices.

In order to listen to a speaker, we begin by hearing and selecting oral messages and taking in the accompanying non-verbal signals. When these messages are interesting or important, we pay attention to them.

We choose to listen because:

- ➤ The message is important
- ➤ We are interested in the information
- ➤ We care
- ➤ We feel like listening
- ➤ We listened to this kind of information in the past
- ➤ We like/respect the person speaking
- ➤ We want to make a good impression

Sometimes, even when we choose to listen, anger, frustration, grief, or fatigue can act as "emotional earplugs." We tend to hear what we expect, or want to hear, and filter out that which is not consistent with our expectations. For example, Jennifer was on her way to lunch when her manager dropped a report on her desk and said he needed 20 sets of copies when he returned from lunch. Jennifer was upset because her friends were waiting and she assumed she had to make the copies immediately. She did not hear her boss say after *his* lunch, which was an hour later than hers. If she had listened carefully, she would have had ample time to make the copies after she returned from her lunch.

Three Keys to Hearing the Message

- ➤ Care
- ➤ Pay attention
- ➤ Select what is important

Listening Lab: Hearing the Message

Exercise 1

Sit quietly someplace where people are talking around you: hotel lobby, office corridor, restaurant, airport. Listen for about 10 minutes then write down what you heard (i.e., what people said, and other incidental sounds or noises).

This activity should make you conscious of the many voices and sounds that bombard you daily. It reminds you that listening begins with hearing, but it is a voluntary activity. Check your answers with those of the author in the back of this book.

1. What did you hear? ______________________________

____

2. How many sounds do you remember? ______________________________

3. What sounds did you remember most easily? ______________________________

____

4. Did your mind wander while you were listening?______________________________

5. Try the experiment again with your eyes closed and see if the results are the same. (You will notice how important your eyes are to listening.)

____

____

Listening Lab: Hearing the Message

Exercise 2

Listed below are some methods for improving listening at the "hearing" level. Write any others you can think of. Select one specific method to work on for the next three days. At the end of the three days, assign yourself a grade (A, B, C, D, F) for how well you did.

- Improving your listening vocabulary so that words and meanings are clear when you listen.
- Having your hearing checked.
- Asking for repetition or clarification.
- Overcoming a tendency to daydream.
- Eliminating distractions.

Others:

- ____
- ____
- ____
- ____
- ____

Key Element 2: Interpret the Message

Interpreting a speaker's message means coming to a mutual understanding of the speaker's meaning. Good listeners know that a match-up in meaning is a match-up in understanding. The word "communication" comes from the Latin root word *communis* which means "commonness," a commonness of understanding.

Listeners often experience problems at the interpreting level because no two people perceive information in the same way. Speakers do not always say exactly what they mean, or mean exactly what they say.

What is the difference?

> "*When I look at you, time stands still.*"
>
> "*You have a face that would stop a clock.*"

We probably do not interpret accurately in most listening situations. Listening is a complicated process. Speakers send messages to listeners both verbally and non-verbally. If Jim tells Rod, "You have to do something about the Doughty account," Rod must assign meaning to Jim's words, filters, tone of voice, and non-verbal cues.

Words

Words themselves have little meaning. They are merely vehicles for the thoughts and feelings of the speaker. Words are not actual experiences, but a means of explaining experiences. It is people who give meaning to words.

Filters

Both listeners and speakers have mental filters, which help or hinder the interpreting process. These filters are in our brain's "database," and they attach personal meaning to information. Some examples of filters include the following; *can you add others?*

- memories
- biases
- expectations
- current attention span
- values
- feelings
- language and vocabulary
- age
- assumptions
- perceptions
- attitudes
- emotional hot-buttons
- past experiences
- knowledge and intelligence
- self-esteem
- needs and motives
- sensory acuity

Tone of Voice

Voice conveys approximately 30% of the meaning of a message. Voices can be calm, insistent, pleading, questioning, whining, demanding, etc. Think of tone as the "mood" of the voice. Tom speaks in a quiet monotone. Even though he is intelligent, his voice lacks conviction, and people don't take him seriously. What could Tom do with his voice to get people to listen to him?

Non-verbal Cues

A non-verbal cue, or body language, is a message sent by such things as a speaker's gestures, facial expressions, eyes, and posture. Good listeners interpret a speaker's non-verbal feedback through five channels: ears, eyes, heart, mind, and intuition. Non-verbal cues, along with tone of voice, confirm or deny the message of the words. More than half of most human interaction is through non-verbal communication.

Three Keys to Interpreting the Message

- Understanding your filters
- Listening to the tone of a message
- Recognizing non-verbal signals

Listening Lab: Interpreting the Message

Exercise 1.

Imagine that you have just interviewed a young woman for an important sales position in your department. As she is leaving she remembers one last thing, and states: "By the way, I graduated in the top 10% of my class." Then she shakes your hand, thanks you for the interview, and leaves. Following are some interpretations of her statement. Read these, then list other possible interpretations.

"By the way, I graduated in the top 10% of my class."

1. She is intelligent
2. She is competitive.
3. The school was not academically challenging.
4. She studied constantly.
5. She is bragging.
6. ______________________________
7. ______________________________

How would you clarify your interpretation?

____

____

Listening Lab: Interpreting the Message

Exercise 2.

Say the following sentence out loud seven times.

"I never said you stole the money."

Each time you say it, emphasize a different word. For example, the first time through, emphasize the word "I." I never said you stole the money.

This example shows how voice emphasis influences our interpretation of information. To become a better communicator, listen carefully to the speaker's voice inflection and word emphasis.

Good listeners want to understand the speaker's meaning. They are aware of their own filters and those of the speaker, and they ask questions when they need clarification.

Key Element 3: Evaluate the Message

Good listeners make sure they have all of the key information before forming an opinion. They do not jump to conclusions based on a bias or incomplete information. They may agree with the speaker, or they may disagree. Good listening does not mean automatic compliance. A good listener will weigh and analyze all of the evidence before reaching a final decision or making a written or verbal judgment.

Diana is a member of a jury trying a felony case. As each attorney sifts through the evidence, Diana listens carefully for validation of her opinions. She recognizes her personal biases but seeks to remain objective. She is careful not to jump to conclusions based on emotional testimony. At the end of the trial Diana evaluates all the evidence presented by both sides before making a statement about her decision. The jury foreman later thanks Diana for her valuable observations and objective comments.

We make conscientious evaluations when we make decisions based on all of the available information. We run into problems with evaluation when we think mechanically or jump to conclusions. We must ask ourselves if we are listening to someone or listening against that person. Are we evaluating or making a value judgment?

Evaluation is not required in every listening situation; therefore, we must also know our purpose for listening.

Three keys to Evaluating the Message

- Ask questions.
- Analyze the evidence.
- Don't jump to conclusions.

LISTENING LAB: EVALUATING THE MESSAGE

You listen constantly to advertising on radio and television, and the Internet provides a barrage of information, some of it reliable, some questionable. How often do you stop to evaluate the slant or bias of advertisers who want you to buy their services or try their products? How often do you ask if the information is reasonable and logical? Do you ask yourself what they are not telling you? Following is a description of Adolph Hitler, as it may have been written by his press agent. Read the description as if you were listening to it, taking note of the press agent's built-in bias. Then answer the questions that follow.

"Our leader had an unhappy childhood and little formal education. His father bitterly opposed his ambition to become an artist. Through self-education, he became the author of a book that became a national bestseller. Obstacles do not discourage him. When others say, 'It's impossible,' he hurdles each barrier as it comes. He has built an active youth movement of selected young people. He is known throughout the world for his dynamic speeches. His closest associates say of him, 'He accomplishes incredible deeds out of the passion of his will in order to create the kind of government he believes in.'"

1. How would you evaluate Hitler if you had not heard of him before you read this description? ______________________________

____

2. Are any character flaws suggested in the description? ______________________________

____

3. What methods does the press agent use to create a positive impression of Hitler? ______________________________

____

4. How can this exercise help you evaluate information more carefully?

____

Key Element 4: Respond to the Message

Although a response may be considered a speaking rather than a listening role, it is critical to clear communication. The listener must let the speaker know by verbal and/or non-verbal feedback what was heard and how it was heard.

Good listeners accept responsibility to provide feedback to the speaker to complete the communication process. Good listeners have a strong desire to reach a common understanding.

Responsible responses inform the speaker that:

- ➤ The message was heard.
- ➤ It was understood.
- ➤ It was evaluated appropriately.

Several problems can occur at this point. One is when no response occurs. If Karla asks Jack when the plans for the office remodel will be available, and Jack simply stares at Karla without indicating that he heard her, he is not communicating effectively. Although silence can communicate, a blank stare is not a helpful response. Other problems include responses that are defensive, overly emotional, or inappropriate. If Jack had changed the subject abruptly, his response would have been inappropriate also. Finally, a confusing response (i.e., a double message) can occur when the verbal and non-verbal are in conflict.

If Jack had smiled in a friendly manner, but his voice sounded hostile as he replied, "Why do you want to know?" he would have confused Karla. He was sending her two messages: one with his voice and one with his smile. Double messages are difficult to decode. They are often sent by someone who is afraid of the consequences of telling the truth.

Three Keys to Responding to the Message

- ➤ Seek a common understanding
- ➤ Acknowledge what you hear
- ➤ Avoid confusing messages

Listening Lab: Responding to the Message

Following are several possible responses in listening situations. Place a check mark (✔) next to those you think are important for good communication.

- ❑ Providing prompt feedback
- ❑ Giving feedback that is relevant to the conversation
- ❑ Changing the subject
- ❑ Checking your email
- ❑ Using appropriate eye contact
- ❑ Combining verbal and non-verbal (body language) feedback for more complete communication
- ❑ Staring blankly
- ❑ Asking a question for clarification
- ❑ Mumbling

Add your own responses below:

____

____

Review Lab For Key Elements 1–4

Review each of the key elements in the listening process. Then make a date for coffee with a co-worker and carefully notice yourself going through the four steps when it is your turn to listen.

After your coffee date, the following checklist will help you focus on each key element and evaluate your awareness of your listening behavior. Put a check mark (✔) next to each answer that applies to you.

Review Lab for Key Element 1: Hearing the Message

During our conversation, did I

- ❏ care about my co-worker's attitudes, opinions, and beliefs?
- ❏ pay close attention?
- ❏ ask for clarification when I didn't understand something?
- ❏ allow myself to become distracted?
- ❏ seek to understand the feelings behind the words?
- ❏ listen carefully enough to remember what my co-worker said?

Three specific points made by my co-worker:

____

____

____

Review Lab for Key Element 2: **Interpreting the Message**

During our conversation, did I

- ❑ notice any words that were used in an unusual context?
- ❑ ask questions for clarification?
- ❑ pay attention to his or her tone of voice?
- ❑ watch for non-verbal cues such as facial expression or gestures?
- ❑ notice if the body language, tone, and words all conveyed the same message?
- ❑ let my own filters interfere with my co-worker's meaning?

Two questions I asked in order to make sure that I understood my co-worker's meaning:

____

____

Review Lab for Key Element 3: **Evaluating the Message**

During our conversation, did I

- ❑ believe everything I heard?
- ❑ agree with everything I heard?
- ❑ disagree agreeably?
- ❑ weigh and analyze all of the information before responding?
- ❑ jump to conclusions?
- ❑ ask questions when I needed more information?
- ❑ evaluate the information rather than judge the person?

I evaluated two of my co-worker's statements as follows:

____

____

Review Lab for Key Element 4: Responding to the Message

During our conversation, did I

- ❑ take responsibility for my responses?
- ❑ look and act interested?
- ❑ repeat information for clarity?
- ❑ rush the speaker?

I took responsibility for my responses in the following ways:

____

____

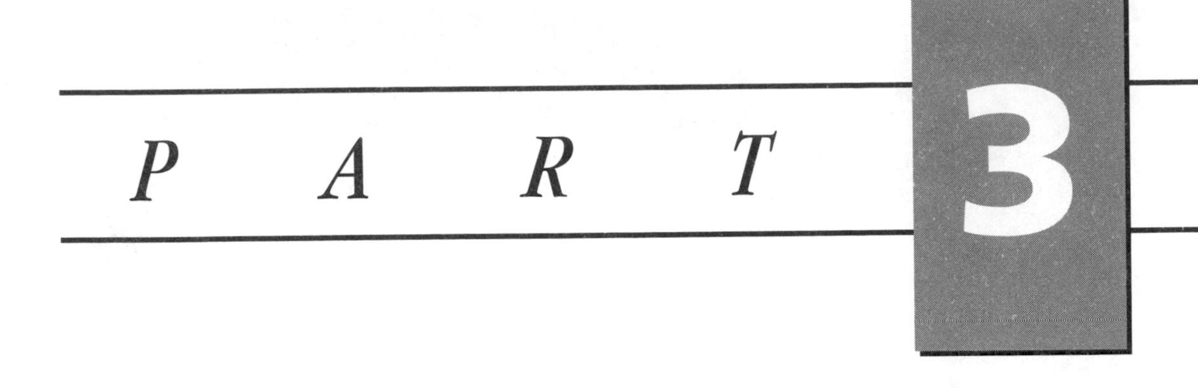

PART 3

Your Listening Style

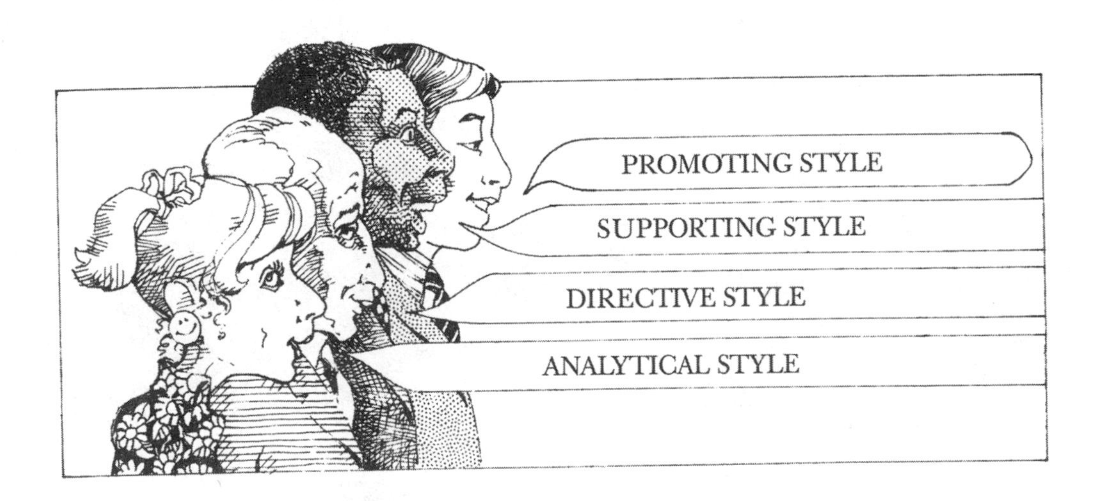

You Are Unique

Each of us has a personal view of how the world should turn. Your personal values, beliefs, attitudes, and behaviors combine to make up your unique style. In this section, four different styles of listening will be examined. They are:

- ➢ **The Promoting Style**
- ➢ **The Supporting Style**
- ➢ **The Directive Style**
- ➢ **The Analytical Style**

Following are descriptions of these styles that could apply to how you perceive information, communicate, and act. Naturally, your style influences the way you listen. When you have read the descriptions, decide which of the four styles comes closest to your preferred method of listening and communicating in general.

Note: No one is just one style. We are combinations of all of the styles, but you will probably see more of yourself in one style than the others. Often we see other people's styles (co-workers, family, friends) before we recognize our own. Don't get locked in here. This information has real value in helping you to understand more clearly your needs and expectations as a listener.

The Promoting Style

The Good Stuff:

These folks are peppy! They have lots of energy and they get excited about things. Their positive outgoing natures motivate everyone. As team members, promoters see the "big picture." They are inventive, confident, and idealistic about reaching goals. In meetings they keep things stirred up by cracking jokes and injecting ideas (even when they aren't asked for). The promoting style is sociable and fun to be around.

The Downside:

Promoters are always on the leading edge with new ideas, but they aren't good at following through. They prefer to leave the grunt work to someone who enjoys that sort of thing. They tend to over-promise, which causes them to be late a lot. A promoter's screensaver might read: "Deadlines amuse me." Some people see promoters as superficial because they move so quickly from idea to idea, without following through. They also appear to be disorganized.

TIPS FOR BETTER LISTENING:

If you have a promoting style, you have a strong personality. Toning down your style and forcefulness can make you less intimidating to others. You don't do well at tolerating indirect communication, so be patient (this is important), and ask questions to understand the meaning.

Because of your attention-getting style, you will have trouble giving up your preoccupation with yourself. To be a good listener you must seek first to understand, then seek to be understood. Some people will perceive your bubbly enthusiasm as insincere and too much "pie in the sky." Balance your energetic style with common sense, and be realistic about keeping promises. If you say you will meet a deadline, do it. You don't have to give up your style in order to be a good listener, but if you match your style to that of the speaker, you will communicate more effectively.

What Gets a Promoter's Attention?

If you want a promoter to listen to you, speak loudly and clearly, use big gestures, paint visual pictures, and lose the detail! You won't hold their attention for long, so plan what you will say and use humor (if you are funny). Include small talk, and don't back away from conflict. (They usually enjoy it.) It's easier to get their attention if you meet with them in a private conference room and their cell phones are out of reach.

LISTENING PROFILE

If you see yourself as a promoting style, answer the following questions:

- ❏ Why do you identify yourself as a promoting style?
- ❏ Based on your style, what are your current strengths as a listener?
- ❏ Based on your style, what are your current weaknesses as a listener?
- ❏ What do you like for people to do or say in order to show that they are listening to you?
- ❏ Given the information about your style, how do you plan to improve your listening? (List three behaviors.)

❏ ______________________________

❏ ______________________________

❏ ______________________________

The Supporting Style

The Good Stuff:

These folks give new meaning to the word "nice." Their friendly helpful style makes them the ultimate team players. They are easy-going and spontaneous, and they take things as they come. They prefer to work in groups and make decisions by consensus. Their decisions are based on the effects their actions will have on others. In meetings the supporting style is a peacemaker who seeks to make co-workers comfortable and happy. Their screensavers might say, "How may I help you?"

The Downside:

Because of their need for acceptance, supporting styles don't always say what they think. They will vacillate in order to please people. They don't do well at setting personal goals. They would rather help other people reach *their* goals. This style operates more on feelings than facts, and they fight with feelings as well.

More forceful styles see supporting styles as easy marks because they can't say no. This style also tends to waste time because they are very social, and they don't take initiative to get things done.

TIPS FOR BETTER LISTENING:

As a supporter, you do a lot of listening. However, you are more tuned to feelings than facts. So you must listen carefully when facts are involved–which is most of the time. Take notes and ask questions for clarification. Be sure to provide feedback on what you hear, then act quickly and responsibly to fulfill your commitments. Learn to say no–a legitimate response at times. Set limits with people on the amount of time you will spend listening, especially if you have work to do; for example, "I can spend five minutes with you, then I need to finish this order." Learn to be assertive and to face dominant personalities without backing down. Listen to them, paraphrase, then state your opinion clearly and directly. These actions will gain their respect.

What Gets a Supporter's Attention?

This one is easy. Supporters are natural listeners because they want to please. If your style is more forceful, tone it down and speak quietly and casually. Engage in small talk and be willing to add a personal touch to your discussion. The supporting style tends to listen more for feelings than facts, so include feelings with facts, such as, "I'd sure feel good about having this report on my desk by three o'clock." Be specific about facts–especially deadlines–because time gets away from supporters very quickly. Ask for confirmation of information to be sure they heard you correctly. It doesn't hurt to check in on a supporter's progress on a project. They enjoy the attention, and it keeps them on track.

Quietly praise their work with gentle "feeling" words. "I liked the way you handled that call." The supporting style doesn't adapt easily to change, so give plenty of warning when changes are going to occur.

LISTENING PROFILE

If you see yourself as a supporting style, answer the following questions:

- ❑ Why do you identify yourself as a supporting style?
- ❑ Based on your style, what are your current strengths as a listener?
- ❑ Based on your style, what are your current weaknesses as a listener?
- ❑ What do you like for people to do or say in order to show that they are listening to you?
- ❑ Given the information about your style, how do you plan to improve your listening? (List three behaviors.)

- ❑ ______________________________
- ❑ ______________________________
- ❑ ______________________________

The Directive Style

The Good Stuff:

Like a human bulldozer the directive style plows through obstacles, ignores excuses, and gets things done. This non-emotional take-charge style approaches problems realistically and boldly. They dominate and control because of their forceful natures. With a director, winning is everything. These hard chargers don't waste time or money, and they are realistic about both. When situations get tough, they tighten the controls. They value achievement and expect big rewards (yachts, money, islands). Their screensavers might say, "What's the bottom line?"

The Downside:

Directors aren't very humble. They have big egos and they play to win. They seldom praise or give credit to others. Sometimes they are downright critical and insensitive. They expect a lot, and they are critical and demanding when they don't get results. Generally they are not good listeners.

Tips for Better Listening:

If you have a Directive style, you are a good listener who doesn't listen. Patience. Patience. Patience. This commodity is in short supply in Director Land, so make it a top priority. Develop enough humility to admit that lots of folks have good ideas, but that a forceful style intimidates them. You use intimidation because you don't want to be used by those who have your ear.

Lighten up and set aside more time for listening to your co-workers, family, and friends. Try style flexing to become more approachable. When you hear a good idea, give credit, even praise. You don't suffer fools lightly, but people with good ideas don't always express themselves well. Again, patience. Ask for feedback; be sensitive; ask for advice from time to time.

What Gets a Director's Attention?

First make an appointment and plan what you will say. Organize your ideas. They will give you five minutes; you give them the bottom line. Anticipate questions and be prepared with sensible persuasive answers. Deal in accurate facts and figures. Don't beat around the bush. (You won't have time for that anyway.) Support your arguments and point of view with logic and realistic data. Forget small talk unless he or she initiates it, then keep it to a minimum. When directive styles listen to you and like what you have to say, they are likely to act quickly and boldly to implement your ideas (for which they may take the credit).

LISTENING PROFILE

If you see yourself as a directive style, answer the following questions:

- ❑ Why do you identify yourself as a directive style?
- ❑ Based on your style, what are your current strengths as a listener?
- ❑ Based on your style, what are your current weaknesses as a listener?
- ❑ What do you like for people to do or say in order to show that they are listening to you?
- ❑ Given the information about your style, how do you plan to improve your listening? (List three behaviors.)

- ❑ ________________________________
- ❑ ________________________________
- ❑ ________________________________

The Analytical Style

The Good Stuff:

This style is, above all, logical! They are usually neat, organized, and precise, and they lean toward professions that require these qualities–engineering, science, accounting, research, and others. As excellent problem solvers they contribute to their work teams with a thorough knowledge of the subject, an objective analysis of available information, and a practical game plan.

They prefer to spend their time with other experienced knowledgeable people. They keep agreements and meet deadlines on time. They are dependable and patient. And did I mention logical?

The Downside:

With so many positive qualities it is hard to imagine a downside to this style. That depends on whom you talk to. Some would say that rightness can turn quickly to self-righteousness, and insistence on complete accuracy soon becomes tedious and boring. Stubbornness becomes an art form, and the push for perfection makes them ever so picky about the smallest details. Their screen-savers might read: "I'm right. I'm right. I'm right."

TIPS FOR BETTER LISTENING:

Your security is in being right. If you don't get this confirmation, you soon tune out. Resist the temptation and keep listening. Learn to accept other people's ideas as valid. Find the logic and truth in their points of view. Develop a sense of humor. The world is a pretty funny place.

You aren't much of a risk-taker, so open your mind to new ideas and be willing to stretch your imagination. Your fear of being wrong makes you stubbornly resistant to listening to information that contradicts your point of view. There's more than one way to peel a potato, so listen louder. As they say, even a broken clock is right twice a day.

What Gets an Analyzer's Attention?

Rule one: make sense. Be logical and organized in your presentation, and be prepared to support your data with facts–lots of them. Keep small talk to a minimum, as analyticals are quiet internal people who consider small talk a waste of time. And they aren't very good at it themselves. Sprinkle your conversations with phrases like, "You're right about that," and, "You sure figured that one out in a hurry." "I hadn't thought of that," works too, because you probably hadn't. If analytical styles don't respond to your questions right away, they're thinking, so give them the time they need. They will reward you with a reasonable well-thought-out answer.

LISTENING PROFILE

If you see yourself as an analytical style, answer the following questions:

- ❑ Why do you identify yourself as an analytical style?
- ❑ Based on your style, what are your present strengths as a listener?
- ❑ Based on your style, what are your present weaknesses as a listener?
- ❑ What do you like for people to do or say in order to show that they are listening to you?
- ❑ Given the information about your style, how do you plan to improve your listening? (List three behaviors.)

❑ ____________________

❑ ____________________

❑ ____________________

OPTIONAL PRACTICE

With a friend, co-worker, or a small group, discuss the different communication styles. Determine your styles and discuss how they are the same as or different from one another.

If your styles are the same, discuss how they are alike and how you can listen effectively to those whose styles are different.

If your styles are different, discuss how you like to be approached in a conversation and how you like to be listened to.

Don't (do, say, act like) this if you want me to listen ____________________

____

Please (do, say, act like) this if you want me to listen ____________________

____

Discuss what each of you can do to become a better listener.

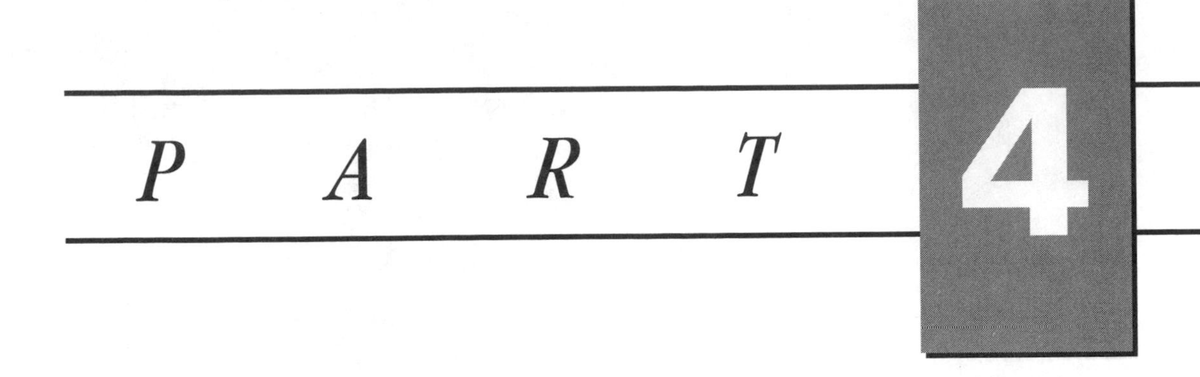

PART 4

What's Your Listening Attitude?

A Listening Attitude: Your Key to Success

What kind of a listener are you? Conscientious? Rushed? Thoughtful? Interruptive? This section provides you with some self-evaluation tools. What is your listening attitude? How well does it contribute to your overall success in business? In your personal life?

Most people believe they are effective listeners. However, as previously noted, research indicates that on average we are effective listeners at only a 25% efficiency level. Much of the time we *think* we are listening. We seem to believe that because we have ears we are listening. This is like believing that because we have eyes we can read. Unconscious attitudes and undiagnosed bad habits such as interrupting, allowing ourselves to be distracted, jumping to conclusions, daydreaming, or giving in to boredom prevent us from becoming the kinds of listeners we think we are. The only way for us to progress is to make some conscious changes.

How well do you listen? Identifying your listening strengths and weaknesses, and deciding which changes you want to make will make you a better listener. To be effective, plan positive action steps, then practice specific listening skills at every opportunity. This will dramatically improve your ability to listen more effectively.

Change begins with an honest self-evaluation of our strengths *and* weaknesses. The exercises in this section will allow you to evaluate your listening attitudes and resulting behaviors so you can plan a strategy for change.

LISTENING LAB: WHAT'S YOUR LISTENING ATTITUDE?

Developing listening skills is an ongoing process. Discovering your attitude about listening is an important first step toward personal success. Attitudes determine our behaviors. To discover your listening attitudes, complete the following exercise. If a statement describes your listening attitude or behavior, put a check mark (✔) under "Yes;" if not, check "No." Be honest.

Listening Attitudes and Behaviors

	Yes	No	
1.	___	___	I am interested in many subjects and do not knowingly tune out dry-sounding information.
2.	___	___	I listen carefully for a speaker's main ideas and supporting points.
3.	___	___	I take notes during meetings to record key points.
4.	___	___	I ignore most distractions.
5.	___	___	I keep my emotions under control.
6.	___	___	I disagree agreeably.
7.	___	___	I wait for the speaker to finish before finally evaluating the message.
8.	___	___	I respond appropriately with a smile, a nod, or a word of acknowledgment as a speaker is talking.
9.	___	___	I am aware of mannerisms that may distract a speaker and keep mine under control.
10.	___	___	I understand my biases and control them when I am listening.
11.	___	___	I refrain from constantly interrupting.
12.	___	___	I value eye contact and maintain it most of the time.
13.	___	___	I often restate or paraphrase what the speaker said to make sure I have the correct meaning.
14.	___	___	I listen for the speaker's emotional meaning as well as subject-matter content.

CONTINUED

CONTINUED

	Yes	No	
15.	___	___	I ask questions for clarification.
16.	___	___	I respect other persons' opinions, even when I disagree.
17.	___	___	When listening on the telephone, I keep one hand free to take notes.
18.	___	___	I attempt to set aside my ego and focus on the speaker rather than on myself.
19.	___	___	I am careful to judge the message rather than the speaker.
20.	___	___	I am a patient listener most of the time.

The following scale will help you interpret your present listening skill level based on your current attitudes and behaviors.

1–5 "No" answers	You are an excellent listener. Keep it up!
6–10 "No" answers	You are a good listener, but can improve.
11–15 "No" answers	Through practice you can become a much more effective listener in your business and personal relationships.
16–20 "No" answers	Listen up!

Barriers to Communication

Our attitudes about certain people or particular subjects greatly affect our listening behavior. Attitude can be a bridge or a barrier to good communication. Listeners can avoid the barriers to listening by understanding the pitfalls and knowing how to avoid them.

Following are descriptions of some listening attitudes. Answer the questions following each description in order to help these "characters" improve their listening behaviors.

Vacant Vincent

The most difficult person to communicate with is a daydreamer. Meet Vacant Vincent. You will recognize him by the faraway look in his eyes. Vincent is like a social butterfly who dips in and out of conversations picking up bits and pieces of information. He is physically present but not really there. Vincent is easily distracted and often changes the subject without warning. Sometimes he slouches, plays with his tie, or impatiently taps his pencil on the desk. The best way to get Vincent's attention is to talk about his interests.

What is Vincent's attitude? ______________________

How can Vincent become a better listener? Following is a list of possible behaviors. Put a check mark (✔) next to any that would help Vincent improve his communication skills.

___ Sitting in a listening position

___ Controlling distractions

___ Fidgeting

___ Taking an interest in other people

___ Making eye contact

___ Reading his email

___ Sticking to the subject

___ Mental channel surfing

Check your answers with those of the author in the back of this book.

Critical Carrie

A good manager listens carefully for the critical facts and the logic that supports them. Critical listening is important in management, especially when problems need to be solved. However, some managers listen in order to find fault. Critical Carrie listens for the facts, but is so critical of each item that she often misses "the big picture." She seldom spends time with her staff, but when she does she is usually issuing orders. She asks abrupt questions and cuts people off before they can respond fully. Her questions are demanding and make her staff feel cornered. Carrie frowns or rolls her eyes in disbelief and is quick to place blame. Critical Carrie is an incessant note taker, so her eye contact is limited. She finds little time for small talk. Her staff wishes she would "lighten up" and not jump to conclusions so quickly. Because she seldom listens to them, her staff avoids her. They long ago stopped sharing information with her because "she doesn't listen anyway."

What is Carrie's attitude? ______________________

What would help Carrie communicate more effectively with her staff? Following is a list of behaviors. Put a check mark (✔) next to any that would help Carrie improve her listening attitude.

___ Building rapport with "small talk"

___ Taking more notes

___ Creating an atmosphere of mistrust

___ Developing patience

___ Listening for the "big picture"

___ Showing interest in her employees

___ Learning karate

___ Learning to smile

Check your answers with those of the author in the back of this book.

Compliant Curtis

Compliant listening is a passive behavior that does not allow the speaker to understand the real feelings or opinions of the listener. Listeners such as Compliant Curtis listen much more than they talk. In many cases, they are shy. They want to please others and keep communications pleasant. Compulsive talkers often seek out listeners like Compliant Curtis, because they need people with the patience to listen to them. Unfortunately, when Curtis speaks, he usually keeps his real opinions to himself for fear of criticism. Sometimes he fakes attention as he silently thinks his private thoughts. In meetings Curtis nods his head approvingly, but adds little to the discussion. You will recognize Compliant Curtis by such phrases as "That's nice," or "I see your point."

What is Curtis's attitude?____________________________________

How can Curtis become a more involved listener? Put a check mark (✔) next to any of the following behaviors that would help him improve his listening style.

___ Working to develop positive assertiveness	___ Daydreaming
___ Listening with intention	___ Asking questions
___ Speaking with conviction	___ Voicing his opinions
___ Avoiding eye contact	___ Agreeing more often

Check your answers with those of the author in the back of this book.

Bridges to Communication

"Active" listening is the bridge to good communication. It is committed listening based on good habits and self-control. Good listening is purposeful and productive because it allows the listener and the speaker to reach an understanding. Following are descriptions of active listening attitudes that create positive communication.

Arlo Active

Arlo Active, a skilled training director, is an involved listener. He is present and participates and assumes responsibility for the success of communications in his department. In meetings and discussions Arlo requires discipline and relevance from his employees and bridges gaps in understanding by asking questions for clarification. He uses humor effectively to break tension and keep things moving smoothly. Individuals in his department appreciate Arlo's clear verbal and non-verbal responses and focused eye contact. Arlo tries to see the other person's point of view, and he refrains from evaluating information too quickly. As an active listener, Arlo listens not only to the content of employees' statements, but also to their intent.

What is Arlo's attitude? ______________________________

See atuhor's comments in back of book.

Lisette Listener

Lisette Listener, a successful real estate agent, credits her success to purposeful listening. When interviewing potential clients, Lisette listens carefully to their requirements for a home. She pays close attention to where they want to live, the desired style of house, and the value they place on schools and services. She asks many questions for clarification. Then she "feeds back" what she hears to be sure she is accurate in her interpretation. By the end of a busy "listening" day Lisette often feels as tired as if she had built a house, rather than sold one. She realizes that active listening is hard work, but she knows her results are measured clearly by her commissions, her satisfied new home owners, and the new friends she makes.

What is Lisette's attitude?____

See atuhor's comments in back of book.

OTHER BRIDGES AND BARRIERS

What other listening attitudes (positive and negative) can you think of? What are some behaviors that support these attitudes?

Listening Attitude	Verbal or Non-verbal Behavior
Positive • • • •	
Negative • • • •	

How Well Do You Listen?

A good way to find out how well you listen is to take a Personal Listening Inventory. This will help you to identify, plan, and practice skills to improve your listening. The Personal Listening Inventory on the next page will help you rate yourself as a listener. An interpretation of results follows this inventory. When you have completed it you will have a better insight into:

- How you rate yourself as a listener
- How you think others rate you as a listener
- How you rate others as listeners

Personal Listening Inventory

1. On average, what percentage of each business day do you spend listening? ____

2. On a scale of 1–10 (with 10 being the highest), how would you rate yourself as a listener? ____

3. On a scale of 1–10, how committed are you to improving your listening?

____

4. On a scale of 1–10, how would you rate the best listener you know?

____

5. On a scale of 1–10, how would you rate the worst listener you know?

____

6. On a scale of 1–10, how would the following people (where appropriate) rate you as a listener?

Manager ____

Subordinate ____

Close colleague ____

Spouse/Lover ____

Child(ren) ____

Best friend ____

For the author's interpretation of the Personal Listening Inventory see the next page.

Personal Listening Inventory: Author's Interpretation

The following interpretation of the Personal Listening Inventory you took on page 57 will help you compare your results with those of others.

1. According to experts, we spend approximately 80% of each business day communicating. Of that time, 45% is spent listening, 30% speaking, 16% reading, and 9% writing. A manager may spend up to 60% of each business day listening.
2. Most people listen at about 50% efficiency. In other words, if tested immediately on what they just heard, they would accurately remember 50%. However, the efficiency rate drops quickly, and most people average a 25% efficiency rate overall.
3. We need to commit to becoming better listeners, because listening is hard work. It requires attention, patience, persistence, and a plan for improvement. Casual involvement and genuine commitment are not the same thing. Suppose you had ham and eggs for breakfast. The chicken was involved in the meal, but the pig was committed. What is your commitment to your listening improvement?
4. Best listeners are usually rated as 8, 9, or 10. This is higher than most individuals rate themselves. The best listeners are often mentors, role models, or professional counselors.
5. Worst listeners are usually rated as 0–4. This score is much lower than most people rate themselves. "Worst listeners" are often related to us, probably because we save our worst behaviors for the people closest to us.
6. It is not unusual to discover that our best friends rate us highest, and our family lowest. Subordinates and colleagues rank us about the same as we rank ourselves. Bosses usually rank us higher than we rank ourselves because we listen better to them than to others. In other words, we are more attentive when there is a direct payoff–or penalty.

Your Listening Qualities: An Awareness Exercise

List five of your best listening qualities, such as patience, good eye contact, not jumping to conclusions, asking for clarification, etc. Rank them 1–5, with 1 being your best quality.

1. ______________________________
2. ______________________________
3. ______________________________
4. ______________________________
5. ______________________________

List three listening qualities that you don't have now but would like to have.

1. ______________________________
2. ______________________________
3. ______________________________

List five of your worst listening qualities, such as impatience, poor eye contact, jumping to conclusions, not asking for clarification, etc. Rank them 1–5, with one 1 being the worst, etc.

1. ______________________________
2. ______________________________
3. ______________________________
4. ______________________________
5. ______________________________

List three listening qualities of poor listeners you know that you would like to avoid. Make a commitment to be more patient with those people and not fall into those behaviors yourself.

1. ______________________________
2. ______________________________
3. ______________________________

How to Stomp Bad Listening Habits

Bad habits are not always easy to break. Following the suggestions below will help you stomp those bad listening habits.

Catch yourself in the act

Recognition is the first step for preventive maintenance. By listing the listening habits you want to eliminate on the previous page, you should be able to recognize them more readily. By monitoring your listening behavior you can catch yourself when you fall into an undesirable behavior, then take steps toward positive change. Remember, you must want to change or you will not make the effort.

Fight the habit

Don't tolerate what you want to eliminate from your listening style. Stomp it. Drop it. Change your ways! Like a smoker kicking the habit, cold turkey is the best way. Don't wait until next time to do things differently. Admit your behavior (i.e., "I just interrupted you. I'm sorry, please go on with what you were saying.") This is a way of catching yourself in the act and acknowledging your bad habit.

Substitute the old habit for a new habit

Memorize the list of new habits you want to develop. If you are chronically impatient, learn patience. For example, think about how you appreciate other people's patience when you are trying to explain something, then act the way you were treated. Visualize yourself as being patient, or not interrupting, or listening without daydreaming, etc. Look for the value in the new behavior you select and trust yourself to do it.

Acknowledge your success

When you substitute an improved listening behavior successfully, give yourself a reward or a pat on the back. Put money toward a vacation fund, or a star in your listening diary. Say to yourself, "I did it!" Tell someone to see if they praise you; or better yet, tell someone you know will praise you.

Be patient with yourself

Why is it that we are more tolerant of other people's mistakes than of our own? Cut yourself some slack. In other words, give yourself a break, and be realistic when you set your listening goals. Self-improvement is a lifelong project, and the road to success is always under construction. There's no such thing as perfect listening, but we can all improve.

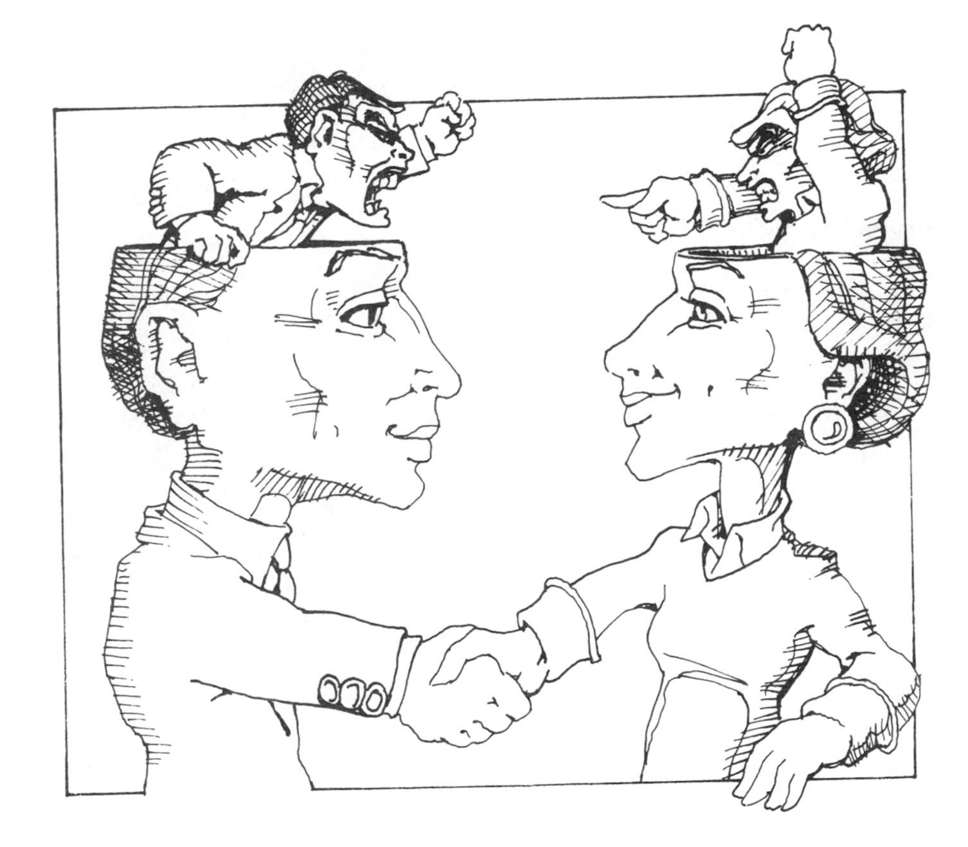

How to Help Someone Listen to You

Much of this book focuses on how you can become a better listener. And although your skills may improve, how do you help others improve their skills? How do you get them to listen to you?

The hard truth is that we can be responsible only for our own listening. If we listen respectfully and model good listening behavior we are more likely to be listened to. However, some people are not attentive listeners, despite your good example. In this case, be assertive and ask them to listen. Ask politely and with good will. If you don't mention the problem, chances are they will continue to listen haphazardly, because poor listeners usually don't know they are doing anything wrong. They are both unskilled and uninformed.

Statements to help people listen:

> *"I feel that I'm not being listened to (heard)."*
>
> *"This information is important and I need to know that you are hearing me. So I need your undivided attention."*
>
> *"Please listen to me."*
>
> *"I feel (ignored, angry, unimportant to you) when you don't listen."*
>
> *"Let me repeat what I just said, as it is important that you hear me."*

Behaviors That Help People Listen

Following are suggestions that may make it easier for others to want to listen to you. Place a check mark (✓) next to those you identify with.

❑ **I am interested in the thoughts and opinions of others.**

People don't care what you know until they know you care. Do you listen to others in the way that you like to be listened to? Don't expect others to listen to you if you are heedless or overly critical of their ideas and attitudes. Respect must be mutual for good communication to thrive.

❑ **I am interesting to talk to.**

I have a few hobbies, go to the movies, read the paper, or like sports. I know what is happening on television and on the Internet. I have traveled. I tell good stories and I know a few jokes appropriate for mixed audiences. I speak clearly and distinctly, and I use good English. I don't repeat myself. I do not sprinkle my vocabulary with colorful epithets (swearing). I have one or two areas of expertise about which I can speak with some authority (carpentry, computers, raising dogs, etc.) I am enthusiastic. I don't speak in a monotone or sound bored. If I am shy, I try to believe in myself and to express my opinions more often. (If you feel that others wouldn't be interested in hearing what you have to say because you are a little boring, take a Dale Carnegie course. It can't hurt.)

❑ **I tell the truth.**

Remember the old adage: "If you tell the truth, you won't have to remember what you said." Everyone has a good "baloney barometer," and exaggeration and white lies are seldom tolerated for long.

❑ **I avoid "bigshotistis" and name dropping.**

Familiar references to famous people or high-ranking officials are appropriate if we know them well; otherwise we are using their names to make ourselves look important. Putting ourselves in a "one-up" position means that the listener is in a "one-down" position. Then communication becomes competition.

❑ **I am my authentic self.**

You are the first-best you, and the second-best anyone else. Being comfortable with being you is the greatest gift you can give yourself. You are unique. Let that be enough. Pretense is a result of trying to be like someone else because we don't like who we are. When we are settled with ourselves, others find us more approachable and likable.

❑ **I am conscious of timing and preliminary tuning.**

I prepare my listener for what I am going to say. For example: "You should know the counts for both kinds of cholesterol when you have your cholesterol level tested. Let me say why I think that." Be aware of the processing time needed by your listener. Be patient. Some people are internal processors and take extra time to think before they respond. External processors may answer rapidly, but they might not respond as clearly or accurately.

❑ **I get to the point. Keep the message moving.**

Too much detail kills interest. Keep your listener stimulated by providing new ideas, adding colorful words, anecdotes, and visual images. Avoid jargon, clichés, and hackneyed phrases. Be specific and be clear. Don't repeat yourself. Don't force assumptions. Fill in the background, but avoid endless detail. When possible, plan what you will say to make it easy for your listener.

❑ **I am sensitive to my listener's needs.**

Don't drop verbal grenades when the listener is in the wrong physical or psychological state. Break bad news gently. It isn't what you say, it is how you say it. Outline your message. "Our financial picture is somewhat bleak for next quarter. Here are three ideas for coping with the problem." Say the vital parts first and last. People seldom remember what is in the middle.

❑ **I use my listener's name regularly.**

People love to hear their own names. Use them often in your communication and give others credit for their ideas and suggestions. Ask them questions and seek feedback about their opinions.

❑ **I use good eye communication.**

Really seeing people is very different from just looking at them. Use verbal and non-verbal signals to let your listeners know that you want to talk with them, rather than at them. Take the time to evaluate your communication skills honestly. Our personal attitudes, habits, and intentions greatly affect the way others listen to us.

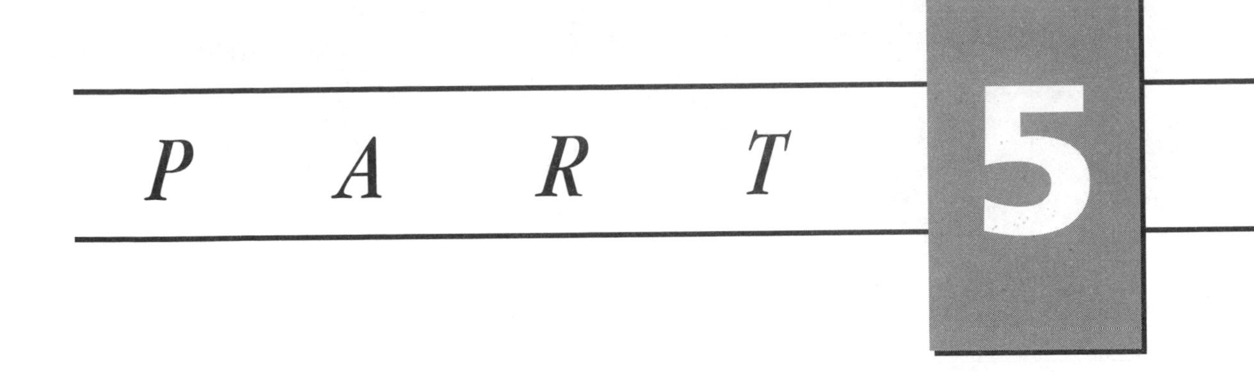

PART 5

Ten Tips for Tip-Top Listening

Listening Louder

Listening is both a behavior and a skill. Behavior is evidence of our ability to apply a skill. To improve our listening skills we need to consciously practice the 10 tips in this section. A good driver does more than simply avoid accidents, and a good listener does more than simply pay attention.

Because business is a place where you need to listen most of the time, you will have plenty of opportunity to practice. Mentally condition yourself to make every encounter, from your first phone call to the last meeting of your business day, an opportunity to practice improved listening. Be practical and select the tips that will help you the most.

The following tips will help you "listen louder." Consciously select those you wish to work on, then establish a list of listening priorities.

Tip 1: Take Notes

Good listeners are note takers. They realize that minds are imprecise and memory is imperfect. Note-taking will help you follow disorganized speakers, help you locate the key points, and identify supporting data. The following suggestions can help you improve your note-taking skills.

Be prepared. Carry a small notepad and a pen at all times. (Some people prefer to carry a small tape recorder.) Use the pad or tape recorder regularly to record any thoughts or ideas you want to remember. Note the speaker, situation, and time. (In selected situations you should ask permission before taking notes, using a laptop computer, or recording what is said. Use good judgment.)

Get it down. Don't take time to be overly neat. If necessary you can recopy your notes later. Write just clearly enough so you remember what you wrote and why you wrote it. Answer the questions: who? what? why? when? and where?

Don't try to write everything. Avoid complete sentences. Write nouns that create visual pictures. Use active verbs. Develop and use your own shorthand including symbols, pictures, punctuation, and abbreviations (e.g., Suzie Hilgeman, lnch w/HP client, Fri. 11:30 @JoJo's).

Tip 2: Listen Now, Report Later

You can improve your listening significantly by planning to report what you heard to someone later. (Taking notes will increase your effectiveness even more.) Think of a co- worker or a friend who would benefit from or enjoy the information you're listening to, and plan to tell him or her what you've learned. Your listening then takes on the added dimension of a rehearsal.

Tip 3: Want to Listen

To be good listeners we must be willing to give up a preoccupation with ourselves. Simply put, we must want to listen. The following memory device describes the skills and attitudes we need to insure our listening success:

To be a good listener, use your DISC drive.

Desire From a desire to listen comes commitment. A committed athlete does not play half of each game. We must want to listen to be effective communicators.

Interest According to the writer G. K. Chesterton, there is no such thing as an uninteresting topic; there are just uninterested people. We must develop an interest in either the person and/or the topic to be good listeners.

Self-discipline We must learn self-discipline to eliminate distractions, understand the speaker's key points, overcome boredom, interpret voice inflection and tone, understand non-verbal cues, and comprehend the main idea. Next time you are in a listening situation, pay attention to how well you control your listening habits. Monitoring your listening behavior is essential to taking positive action later.

Concentration Concentration requires greater effort than does paying attention. You pay attention when you juggle balls, and you concentrate when you juggle eggs. Concentration is focused mental energy, and it is a limited commodity. How long can you concentrate intently in a meeting or on the telephone? Why can some people concentrate for hours, while others grow restless in minutes? Think of concentration as money in the bank. If you are like most people, your money is a limited resource. You must discipline yourself to spend it carefully. You must choose how you spend your concentration energy, as well.

You have more ability to concentrate at some times than at others. Are you more alert in the morning or the afternoon? How well do you concentrate after a heavy meal or a hard day on the job? Take advantage of your maximum ability to concentrate by:

➤ Planning your time

➤ Knowing your limits

➤ Setting listening priorities

To improve your concentration develop an opportunistic attitude. Ask yourself these questions:

➤ Why am I listening?

➤ What can I learn or pass along to a co-worker?

➤ How can I use this information?

Concentration improves when you develop mental pictures of what the speaker is saying. If Joe calls to say that he will have the Wilson report on your desk by 2:30 p.m. on Friday, visualize Joe placing the report on your desk. Notice how Joe is dressed. Imagine the word Wilson in bold letters on the cover of the report. See in your mind a clock that reads 2:30 p.m. next to your desk calendar turned to Friday. By visualizing what you want to remember, you create "dwell time" for your mind to encode the information into your long-term memory.

LISTENING LAB: CONCENTRATION CHECKLIST

Complete the following exercise to identify some reasons why you do not always concentrate.

Rate the following items that apply to you using a scale from 0–3, with 0 being no problem; 1 being a minor problem; 2 being somewhat of a problem; and 3 being a major problem. Total your score and compare it to the box at the end of the exercise.

___ I'm in a hurry.

___ I become distracted by what is going on around me.

___ I'm self-conscious.

___ I'm bored.

___ I'm thinking about what I'm going to say next.

___ I'm in surroundings that are "out of my comfort zone."

___ I already know what the speaker is going to say.

___ I'm used to having things repeated.

___ I'm on mental overload most of the time.

___ I'm not responsible for the information.

___ I'm tired.

___ I'm confused by the topic or the speaker.

___ I'm daydreaming.

0–5	You have excellent concentration skills.
6–15	This book should help improve your concentration skills.
16 or more	You need a specific action plan to improve concentration skills, and you need a good rest.

Tip 4: Be Present

Like it or not, we always choose whether or not we will listen. When we choose not to listen, our minds are on vacation and we do not interpret, evaluate, or respond appropriately to the speaker and the message. Only when we choose to "be present" are we focused on the speaker and the message.

Our number one alternative to being present is daydreaming. Daydreaming is a comfortable private escape. It normally doesn't disturb anyone, and often others don't realize we're doing it. Daydreaming is what we elect to do when we choose not to be present.

Daydreaming is the single greatest barrier to active listening. To be present and listen effectively, we must recognize our mental vacations, put them aside, and bring ourselves back to the subject at hand.

The exercise on the next page will help you recognize your "DQ" (Daydream Quotient) and suggest steps to take to be present in your listening.

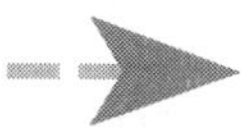

Listening Lab: Your "DQ" (Daydream Quotient)

For this exercise take a piece of paper and make note any time you daydream while reading the rest of this book. If your mind wanders, jot down where it went and what you were thinking about, then quickly return your attention to your reading.

When you complete *The Business of Listening*, review your "DQ" to see if there are repeated subjects or patterns in your daydreams. If so, they may be matters for conscious attention and action.

We All Daydream

We all daydream–many of us as much as 50% of the time. Next time you are in a listening situation, check your DQ to notice how often you mentally wander off while the speaker is talking. If you "wander" at least once per minute, chances are you need more concentration and self-discipline in your listening.

Effective listeners focus on the speaker and listen hard for the content of the message. They avoid the embarrassment of being caught daydreaming. While we are never tested on our daydreams, we can, at any time, be tested on the content of the message.

Tip 5: Anticipate Excellence

Expectations play a powerful role in our lives. How often have we avoided a co-worker because we didn't want to spend time listening to small talk? Other times we may have made up an excuse to miss a speaker we expected to be boring.

By giving others a chance to speak intelligently and by anticipating excellence from them, we can help them become successful. As humans we have a deep and unending need to be heard and understood. When we set aside our needs and truly listen, people will drop their pretenses and speak to us in a more mature and connected manner. See Kathy's story on page 99.

Listeners can help speakers by:

- Asking questions
- Showing interest
- Expressing concern
- Paying attention

People do their best when they know someone is listening.

CASE STUDY: THE PIONEER'S STORY

This story is about early pioneers in covered wagons crossing into the new Oregon Territory. They stopped to rest at a small settlement, and the wagon master spoke to an old man sunning himself in front of the general store.

"Say, Old Timer, what kind of people have settled out here?"

"What kind of people were they where you came from?" asked the old man.

"Well, they were mean, full of mischief, and small minded. That's why we left," said the wagon master.

"Sorry to say, young feller, but that's the kind of folks you'll find out here," replied the old man.

Later in the week another team of wagons pulled into the same town for supplies. This wagon master also stopped in front of the general store and spoke to the same old man sunning on the steps.

"Say, Old Timer, what kind of people have settled out here?"

"What kind of people were they where you came from?" asked the old man again.

"The people we left behind were kind decent people and they were generous. When we left they gave us supplies and helped us load our wagons. We all miss them very much," sighed the wagon master.

"Well, my friend, you've come to the right place, because those are the kind of people you're going to find out here," replied the old man with a kindly smile.

We get what we expect! Anticipate excellence, and it will happen a lot more often than if we assume otherwise.

Tip 6: Become a "Whole Body" Listener

To be effective listeners we must involve the whole body. Not only are our ears tuned in, but so are our eyes, our minds (the intellect), our bodies, our hearts, and our intuition. Good listeners give both non-verbal and verbal signals that they are listening.

A "whole body" listener tunes in by:

- ➤ Conveying a positive encouraging attitude
- ➤ Sitting in an attentive posture
- ➤ Remaining alert, but comfortable
- ➤ Nodding in acknowledgment of the speaker's words
- ➤ Making good eye contact
- ➤ Listening between the lines
- ➤ Looking like a listener

If you have complete rapport you will naturally match the speaker's physical movements, tone of voice, vocabulary, and breathing patterns. Good listeners are in sensory balance with the speaker.

According to Albert Mehrabian, a noted expert in human behavior, our communication is 55% non-verbal, 38% inflection and tone, and only 7% words.

If Mehrabian is correct, then most of a spoken message is seen and sensed, and the words are far less important than the non-verbal cues and tone of voice.

Think about your personal mannerisms and behaviors. Do you have any of the following habits that would distract or confuse a speaker?

- Fidgeting
- Blinking
- Biting your lip
- Frowning deeply
- Playing with your hair, tie, or jewelry
- Looking at your watch
- Staring

Stop for a moment and think about these behaviors. Would they distract you if you were the one speaking? If your answer is yes, you need to find a way to modify your behavior. Try the suggestions on the next page.

Listening Lab: Becoming a "Whole Body" Listener

1. Check Your Habits

Briefly write your non-verbal listening responses toward two people you know. Choose one person you enjoy and one person you don't enjoy. Are your responses different? If so, how? If you want to change any of your non-verbal responses to either person use the Change line to state your improvement goal.

Person #1 ______________________________

Response	Description	Change
Posture		
Eye contact		
Facial expression		
Mannerisms		
General attitude		
Voice (verbal response)		

CONTINUED

CONTINUED

Person #2 ____________________

Response	Description	Change
Posture		
Eye contact		
Facial expression		
Mannerisms		
General attitude		
Voice (verbal response)		

2. Consider Non-verbal Encouragement

List five things you can do non-verbally to encourage a speaker.

1.

2.

3.

4.

5.

Tip 7: Build Rapport by Pacing the Speaker

Pacing is a method listeners use to build a positive relationship with a speaker by imitating or mirroring his or her verbal and non-verbal cues. These gestures include breathing, voice rate, vocabulary, favorite phrases, and facial expressions. Of course, if we imitate too closely we will be accused of mimicking, and our attempts to build rapport will be lost.

When pacing, the listener focuses on what the speaker is doing as well as what he or she is saying. The listener then makes a conscious effort to become more like the speaker. The speaker senses the similarities and feels at ease because we are most comfortable with people who are more like us. When others' behaviors are very different from our own, we adjust less easily to their styles.

This technique is not meant to manipulate other people. If your intention is to build rapport, you can do it more easily if you take your attention off of yourself and focus it on the other person. That is the purpose of pacing.

As a listener, you can pace those speaking in any of the following ways:

- ➤ Match your voice rate to theirs. Speed up or slow down as necessary.
- ➤ Change your voice volume to match theirs.
- ➤ Notice and use some of the same words and phrases as the speaker.
- ➤ Approximate the speaker's gestures. Sit forward or back, hands on or off the desk, etc. (Do not be too obvious or you will be noticed. Approximate the gestures.)
- ➤ Breathe at about the same rate, without being too obvious. (If the speaker is a Type A and breathes very fast, be careful not to hyperventilate.)

CHERYL'S STORY

Cheryl was preparing to give a technical speech before a large, important audience. She arrived early at the meeting room to test her slides and adapt to the circumstances of the room. When she turned on the rented projector, the bulb in the machine suddenly burned out. Cheryl looked in the projector case but could not find a replacement. Frantically she searched the building for a maintenance person. She found the maintenance supervisor on the next floor, ambling slowly down the hall. Cheryl rushed to the supervisor, explaining her dilemma in a rapid staccato voice that displayed an obvious urgency.

Bill, the supervisor was low keyed. While Cheryl churned like a buzz saw, Bill spoke no faster than a snail on Valium. Cheryl felt she could count to 10 between each of Bill's words. "I'd - like - to - help - you, - but - I don't - have - a - key - to - the - supply - closet," said Bill in a low, slow, patient monotone. Cheryl continued to buzz and Bill continued to dawdle for another minute.

Suddenly Cheryl remembered something she had read about pacing a speaker, and she decided to give it a try. Gradually she began to slow her speech to match Bill's rate. It was painful for Cheryl to talk so slowly, but Bill became more responsive and more helpful as she became less frantic.

Within minutes Bill remembered someone who had a key, and he volunteered to find the bulb she needed. Cheryl couldn't be sure the pacing made the difference, but within 15 minutes she had the replacement bulb. Bill flashed her a big slow smile as he handed her the bulb, along with a spare, in case the replacement burned out. Cheryl thanked him s-l-o-w-l-y, and smiled back. She had found a new friend.

BYRON'S STORY

Byron was an independent sales representative for a refrigeration company in Alaska. Because of his large territory, Byron made most of his contacts by telephone. Byron had heard of pacing from a friend and decided to try it in his cold calls and follow-up over the phone.

When he called potential customers he listened very carefully to what they said and how they said it. Then as he spoke, he paced their voices, speed, inflection, and vocabulary. With no other variables in his experiment other than pacing, Byron was able to increase his refrigeration equipment sales by 30% over the previous quarter.

LISTENING LAB: PACING THE SPEAKER

To develop an ability to pace effectively, follow these guidelines in the suggested sequence:

1. Practice pacing with a friend. Tell him or her what you are doing first. Have your friend tell you a funny story or describe an interesting place to visit and use varied gestures and facial expressions. Mirror each action and expression to get the feeling for the pacing activity. When you both stop laughing, discuss how successful you were and solicit suggestions for improvement.

2. Next, practice pacing on a friend or family member in a no-risk situation. This time try to remain undetected.

3. Finally, practice on a colleague choosing one or two characteristics to mirror. Be natural and sincere. As you pace and observe, exhibit an attitude of wanting to build rapport.

Rapport is the ultimate tool in producing positive results with others. In business, dealing effectively with people is essential. Rapport can help us achieve success. We build rapport by listening actively and acting on what we learn.

- Focused observation
- Complete flexibility
- Tuned-in listening

Tip 8: Control Your Emotional "Hot-buttons"

Words, issues, situations, and/or personalities trigger us emotionally. When these issues trigger our emotional hot-buttons, verbal messages become distorted, either positively or negatively. Because issues are emotional they create barriers to effective listening. When our hot-buttons are activated, we tune out, distort, or prejudge these emotionally charged messages.

Emotional hot-buttons are intense complex feelings that affect everyone. Each may initiate a different emotional reaction, but our physical responses are similar. If you cannot eliminate your emotional hot-buttons, the best alternative is to develop acceptable responses. The physical triggers warn you that emotions are taking over. When emotional levels go up, objectivity comes down. Problems are never resolved satisfactorily at an emotional level.

To control emotional hot-buttons we must identify what triggers us, understand our responses, and develop behaviors that allow us to listen more carefully and objectively. The three-step method on the next page can help you identify your listening hot-buttons.

LISTENING LAB: IDENTIFYING EMOTIONAL "HOT-BUTTONS"

Step 1

Following are some listening situations and phrases that may cause you to become emotional. Put a check mark (✔) next to those that are hot-buttons for you as a listener, and add others that strongly affect you, positively or negatively.

___ "You never/always ..."

___ Know-it-all attitudes

___ "Shut up!"

___ Bigots

___ Bad grammar

___ "You never listen."

___ Pushy individuals

___ Whining

___ "What you should do is . . ."

Others:

___

___

___

Step 2

Read through the list again and cross out any hot-button issues you are willing to give up, in other words, those you can forget and not let them bother you any more. Chances are you will not cross off many items from your list. This step demonstrates that it is difficult to give up habitual ways of responding to emotional situations.

Step 3

Put a check mark (✔) next to the responses on the following list that describe your physical reactions to emotionally charged issues:

___ Heartbeat increases.

___ Hands feel sweaty.

___ Voice shakes.

___ Chest tightens.

Others:

___

___

___

TEN STEPS FOR CONTROLLING EMOTIONAL "HOT-BUTTONS"

Following is a list of coping skills for preventive maintenance when your hot-button is activated by someone's anger or frustration.

1. Listen attentively without interrupting. Take deep breaths to help you control your physical reactions.
2. Make a conscious choice about your response. You can get angry, try to solve the problem, or ignore it. If you choose to solve the problem, you prevent it from happening again.
3. Acknowledge other people's feelings. Make it okay for them to feel the way they do.
4. Ask objective questions for clarification. Open-ended questions are useful.
5. Try to see the other person's point of view. Agree where you can and feed back what you are hearing.
6. Stick to the subject. Define your problem and don't let other issues interfere.
7. Be patient. Problems don't always have immediate solutions. Be patient with the other person–and yourself.
8. Express your point of view. Don't force proof. Present your evidence without backing the other person into a corner.
9. Explain why. A reasonable explanation can often take the sting out of an emotional issue.
10. Work out a "win-win" plan. Make sure your solution is fair and workable for everyone involved.

For additional suggestions refer to "The Joy of Small Change" on page 10.

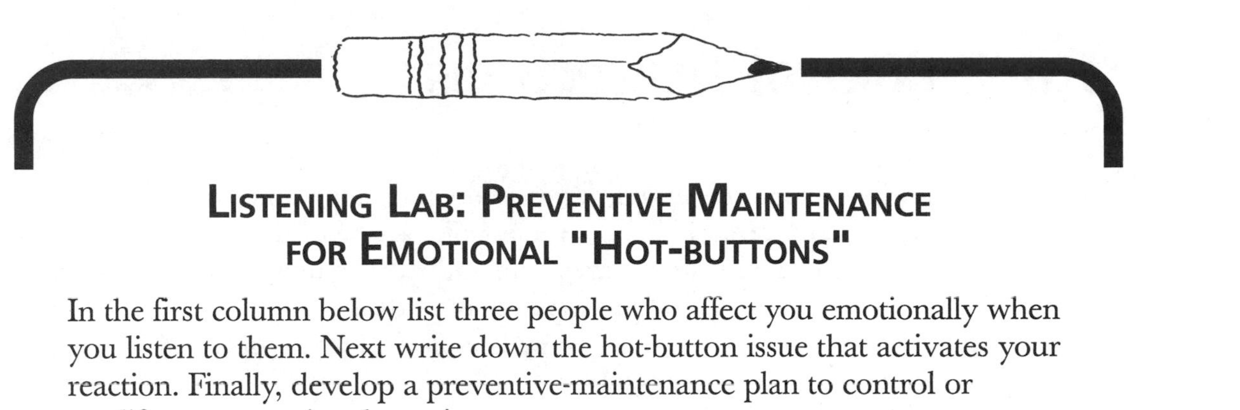

Listening Lab: Preventive Maintenance for Emotional "Hot-buttons"

In the first column below list three people who affect you emotionally when you listen to them. Next write down the hot-button issue that activates your reaction. Finally, develop a preventive-maintenance plan to control or modify your emotional reaction.

	Person	"Hot-button"	Preventive Maintenance Plan
1.	________	________________	____________________________
2.	________	________________	____________________________
3.	________	________________	____________________________

Tip 9: Control Distractions

Comedian George Carlin once asked, "Aren't you glad the phone wasn't invented by Alexander Graham Siren?" A telephone is one of the biggest distractions to listening in a business environment, because unseen others choose when the phone will ring. If the phone were the only distraction, we could probably learn to tolerate it. Every day we must deal with many internal, external, visual, and auditory distractions.

To be good listeners, we must control our responses to distractions or they will control us. Distractions affect the ability to listen well because of their variety, novelty, or intensity. External distractions include the telephone, background noise, unfamiliarity with vocabulary, seating, lighting, etc. Internal distractions might be headaches, hunger, fatigue, or a current emotional state such as anxiety.

STEPHANIE'S STORY

Stephanie was putting the finishing touches on a major marketing presentation when a co-worker called to discuss a budget problem. Stephanie automatically grabbed the phone and answered while still assembling binders. Suddenly she realized her distraction. She told her co-worker politely that she was just finishing a project with a tight deadline and asked if she could return the call in an hour, when the project was completed, so she could be a better listener. By handling the matter this way, Stephanie avoided distraction. She let the caller know her desire to give the budget problem her full attention as soon as possible.

Life and work are full of distractions. Part of our professional responsibility is to manage our working environment. Although our working conditions will never be ideal, we can minimize distractions by taking action to improve our listening, which will help to reduce communication failures.

Listening Lab: Overcoming Distractions

The following statements describe how people might handle various distractions. Place a check mark (✔) next to those items you do well.

- ❑ **Plan your listening.** Don't attempt important business in a restaurant. It's too noisy and you're interrupted frequently. Find a quiet room away from the phone for important meetings. Plan decision-making meetings during your high-energy times of the day. Think about possible distractions and plan to avoid as many as you can.

- ❑ **Do not use distractions as a convenient excuse for not listening.** Overcome distractions with extra concentration and determination.

- ❑ **Identify what is causing a distraction and make adjustments.** Are you too near a noisy copier? Can you move away from it? Do you have a headache? Have you taken an aspirin? Are you hungry? Can you eat an apple? Are the lights too low or too high? Can they be adjusted? Is the phone a problem? Can someone take your calls? In other words, when you have identified the problem, you are one step closer to fixing it.

- ❑ **Ignore the distraction.** If you can't do anything about the distraction, tune it out by concentrating harder. Although you know the distraction is there, focus your attention on the speaker. Use self-discipline.

- ❑ **Call "time out" when you are too tired to listen.** Audial fatigue is caused by constant noise such as fans humming or the drone of machinery or traffic. Intense concentration or physical exhaustion can also cause "ear exhaustion." Don't be shy about calling a halt when you have had enough noise.

Tip 10: Listening Is a Gift, Give Generously

Listening is a skill that anyone can learn. It is also a gift that anyone can give. It is a special gift of a person's time and attention. Listening is an acknowledgment of caring. Honest listening encourages a speaker to be creative and feel more accepted.

According to author Tom Peters, top executives have learned to be excellent listeners. They understand the importance of good listening. The best managers do far more than allow listening to happen. They realize that listening improves effectiveness, accomplishes more, and earns profits.

The gift of listening assumes that the speaker has value, dignity, and something to offer. We must listen every day in the business world. If, in our listening, we take the focus off of ourselves and encourage the speaker to express his or her ideas, we extend a gift that will be repaid many times. Develop a listening attitude. The results are worth it.

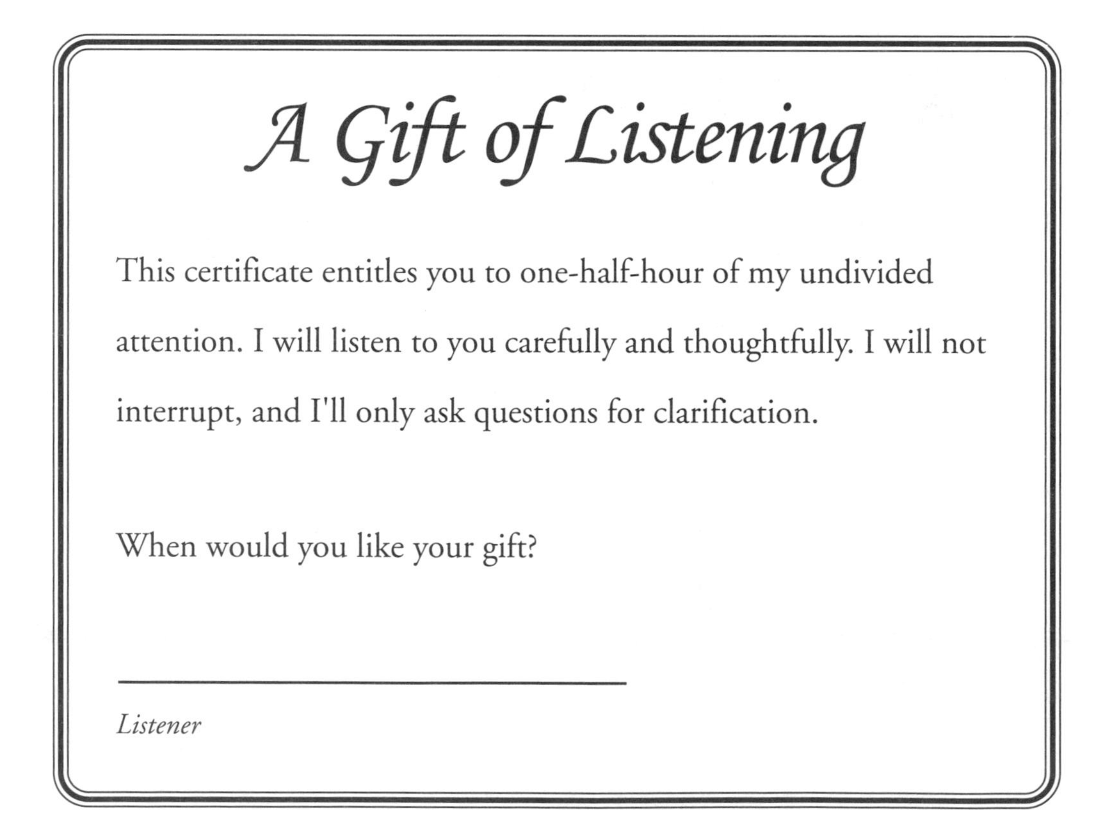

A Gift of Listening
This certificate entitles you to one-half-hour of my undivided attention. I will listen to you carefully and thoughtfully. I will not interrupt, and I'll only ask questions for clarification.
When would you like your gift?
Listener

S U M M A R Y

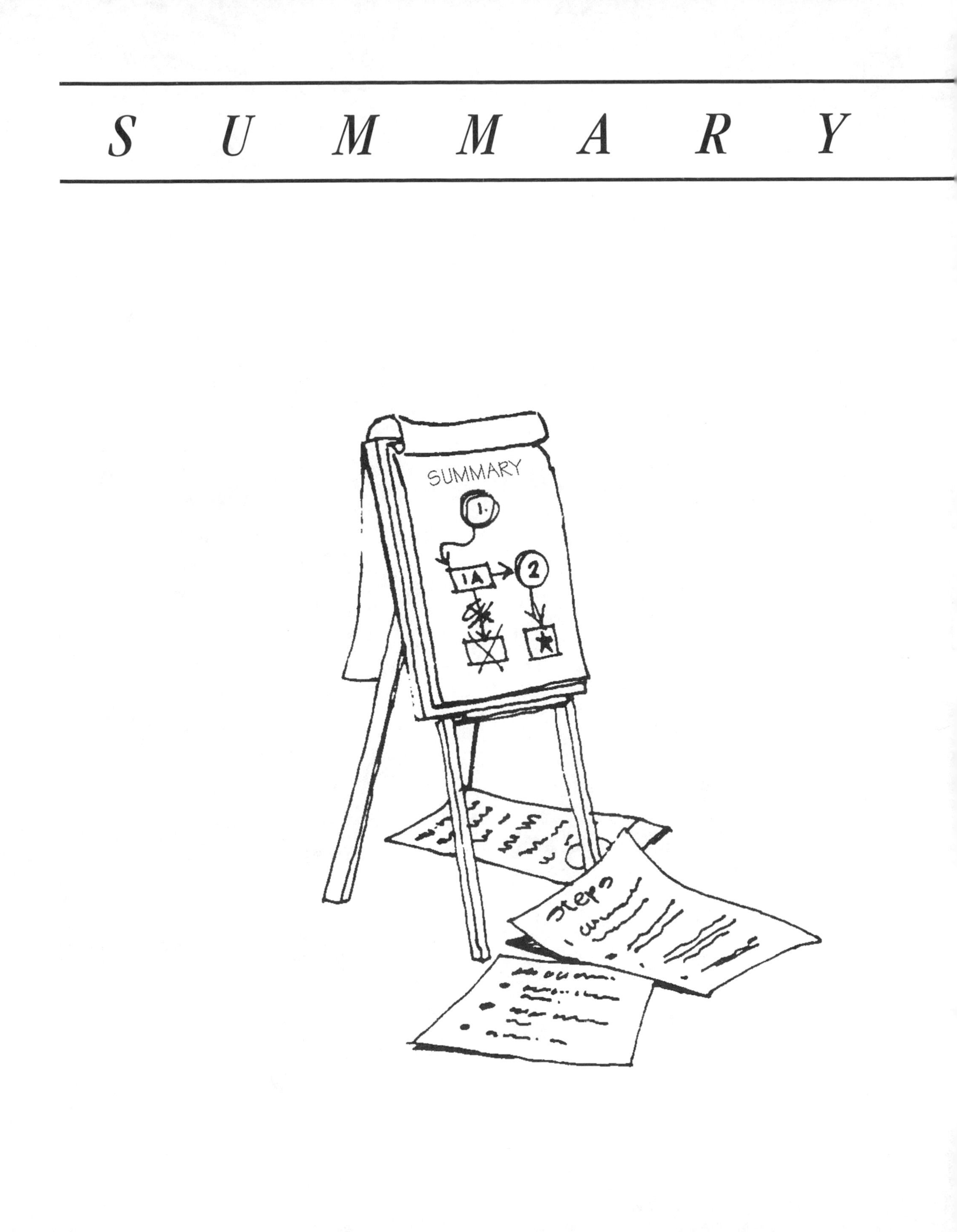

Points to Remember

Following are points to remember from each of the five parts of this book. Review the points to remember then complete your Personal Action Plan. You will be asked to list the listening skills you want to improve, to develop some goals, and to establish a plan to meet those goals.

Part 1: Why Should You Listen?

- ➤ Work and listening are inseparable.
- ➤ Lazy listening is a hidden cost in business.
- ➤ We listen for our own reasons.
- ➤ We can improve listening with desire, motivation, and a plan for constructive change.

Part 2: How to Be a Good Listener

- ➤ Hear the message. Listen to both verbal and non-verbal information.
- ➤ Interpret the message. A good interpretation is a match-up of meaning between the speaker and the listener.
- ➤ Evaluate the message. The listener's opinion should be based on all available information. Ask questions.
- ➤ Respond to the message. Good listening means giving the speaker an appropriate response, verbally and/or non-verbally.

Part 3: Your Listening Style

- Everyone is different.
- Promoting Styles listen for the big picture.
- Supporting Styles listen for feelings.
- Directive Styles listen for the bottom line.
- Analytical Styles listen for facts.

Part 4: Your Listening Attitude—A Barrier or a Bridge?

- Attitude is a choice.
- Positive and negative listening behavior starts with attitude.
- Most people are not good listeners.
- We listen best when there is a payoff or a penalty.
- Personal listening awareness is the key to constructive change.

Part 5: Ten Tips for Tip-Top Listening

- Take notes. They aid retention.
- Listen now, report later. Plan to tell someone what you heard; you will remember it better.
- Want to listen. You must have desire, interest, self-discipline, and concentration to be a good listener.
- Be present. Watch out for the tendency to daydream.
- Anticipate excellence. We get good information more often when we expect it.
- Become a "whole-body" listener. Listen with your ears, your eyes, your heart, your intuition, and your mind.
- Build rapport by pacing the speaker. Approximate the speaker's gestures, expressions, and voice patterns to create comfortable communication.
- Control your emotional "hot-buttons." Knowing what makes you react emotionally is your key to preventive maintenance.
- Control distractions. Controlling internal and external distractions helps you manage your working environment more effectively.
- Give the gift of listening. Listening is a skill, and a gift. Give generously.

Develop a Personal Action Plan

A definition of *accountability* is to be responsible for one's actions. We all have good intentions. What separates those who are successful from those who are not is how well our good intentions are carried out. This Personal Action Plan can convert your good intentions into actions. It is a good starting point if you are serious about improving your listening skills.

1. My current listening skills are effective in the following areas:

2. I need to improve my listening skills in the following areas:

3. I will implement an action plan for listening improvement as follows:

    A. My listening goals:

    B. My plan for reaching my goals:

    C. My timetable:

(Refer to "How to Stomp Bad Listening Habits," page 60, for reinforcement.)

4. The following person(s) will benefit from my improved listening skills:

5. They will benefit in the following ways:

KATHY'S STORY

On Kathy Green's 30th birthday she cautiously invited her parents to join the celebration with a few friends. Her mother had baked Kathy's favorite lemon cake and Kathy felt obligated. However, she was concerned about what the reaction of her friends might be to her parents. Kathy's father was hard-of-hearing and shouted when he spoke. In turn, her mother shouted at her father to tell him what other people were saying. Mrs. Green also talked constantly and changed the subject frequently. Almost any response from her listener would catapult Mrs. Green onto a new topic. Kathy had long since given up really listening to her mother. Kathy's behavior was cool and polite, but non-caring.

Kathy attended a company seminar on listening shortly before the celebration. She realized that although she listened effectively to co-workers, she had developed a habitual "un-hearing" response to her mother.

At her birthday dinner, Kathy began to realize that her mother's behavior was a bid for attention. Mrs. Green was isolated from her husband by his hearing loss and from her only child by Kathy's imposed distancing. It was true that her mother did not have good communication skills, but Kathy realized that her mother changed the topic in an attempt to be more interesting. The more she was rebuffed, the more she changed the subject.

Kathy made a decision following the night of her birthday to pay more attention to her mother. She focused her listening and developed a genuine interest in what her mother was saying. She worked hard to break old listening patterns and substitute new ones. First she noticed only small changes. Her mother began to stick to the subject longer as Kathy asked patient, relevant questions and listened to the answers. At times, Kathy had to guide

CONTINUED

CONTINUED

her mother back to the subject, but she was persistent in her resolve.

After six months Kathy noticed that her mother was calmer and more connected when she spoke. She stopped talking as much and listened with interest as Kathy told her about a recent promotion. True, Mrs. Green still shouted at Mr. Green, but Kathy stopped hearing it as much. Thanks to a simple increase in listening effectiveness, Kathy was able to renew a loving relationship with her parents.

Kathy learned well the business of listening and we hope you are on your way to doing the same. Good Luck!

Author's Suggested Answers and Comments

The Benefits of Listening (page 5)

1. T
2. T
3. T
4. T
5. T
6. F (Committees, meetings, and informal networks are strong evidence that most decisions are made by groups.)
7. T
8. F (Most surveys rank listening as one of the three most important skills of top managers.)
9. T
10. F (Good listeners know how to control distractions by eliminating or ignoring them.)

What Do You Know About Listening? (page 8)

1. F. (Facts are only part of most messages. Good listeners listen for opinion, emotion, and distortion as well.)

2. T. (To listen well, open your eyes, use your brain, your heart, and your intuition.)

3. F. (Hearing is the first step, but you must also interpret, evaluate, and respond to the message.)

4. F. (Paying attention is important, but you must also be able to understand the message, and you must care about the person and/or the message.)

5. F. (Many people pride themselves in being able to "multi-task," but the more you try to do, the more you scatter your attention. Good listening is focused attention.)

6. T. (Your body and mind and spirit work together. If your body is slumped and lumpy, it gives the mind and spirit the same signals. Remember your parents' and teachers' admonitions: "Sit up and listen!")

7. T. (Most can, but not all. If you are distracted, mention it, move, or do something about it. When that doesn't work, ignore it.)

8. F. (Yes, memory is an "overlay" of listening, but you may need to remember something for only a short time. We can't consciously remember everything we heard in the past, but if we were able to listen and act on the information effectively at the time, we were listening.)

9. F. (Listening is anything but passive. Your eyes dilate, your palms perspire, and your body is erect. Your mind is active and your energy is focused.)

10. F. (If the speaker says something you do not understand, interrupt politely and ask for clarification. Otherwise, you will lose the meaning of what follows. Taking notes helps.)

Listening Lab: Hearing the Message (page 18)

1. We hear sounds constantly, but remember few.

2. We remember sounds that are important, interesting, or unusual.

3. Same as #2.

4. We all daydream frequently. We cannot remember what we did not hear.

5. People sometimes complain they cannot listen as well when they are not wearing glasses because they cannot see the speaker's non-verbal message.

Vacant Vincent (page 50)

Attitude: "I don't want to be involved."

Answers: 1, 2, 3, 6, 7

Critical Carrie (page 51)

Attitude: I know all the answers.

Answers: 1, 2, 4, 7, 8

Complaint Curtis (page 52)

Attitude: I don't want to be criticized.

Answers: 1, 2, 4, 5, 7.

Arlo Active (page 53)

Author's Note: Effective listening is important to me and to my job.

Lisette Listener (page 54)

Author's Note: Effective listening pays big dividends.

Additional Reading

Bozek, Phillip E. *50 One-Minute Tips to Better Communication.* Menlo Park, CA: Crisp Publications, 1998.

Burley-Allen, Madelyn. *Listening: The Forgotten Skill* (Self-Teaching Guide). New York: John Wiley & Sons, 1995.

Condrill, Jo and Bennie Bough. *101 Ways to Improve Your Communication Skills Instantly.* Beverly Hills, CA: Goal Minds, 1999.

Devereaux, Rochelle. *Power Listening* (audio cassette). Salem, OR: Business Efficancy, 1997.

Decker, Bert. *The Art of Communicating.* Menlo Park, CA: Crisp Publications, 1996.

Robinson Kratz, Abby. *Effective Listening Skills.* Toronto, ON: Irwin Professional Publishing, 1995.

Now Available From

CRISP. Learning™

Books•Videos•CD-ROMs•Computer-Based Training Products

If you enjoyed this book, we have great news for you.
There are over 200 books available in the ***Fifty-Minute*™ *Series*.**
To request a free full-line catalog, contact your local distributor or
Crisp Learning
1200 Hamilton Court
Menlo Park, CA 94025
1-800-442-7477
CrispLearning.com

Subject Areas Include:

Management
Human Resources
Communication Skills
Personal Development
Marketing/Sales
Organizational Development
Customer Service/Quality
Computer Skills
Small Business and Entrepreneurship
Adult Literacy and Learning
Life Planning and Retirement

CRISP WORLDWIDE DISTRIBUTION

English language books are distributed worldwide. Major international distributors include:

ASIA/PACIFIC

Australia/New Zealand: In Learning, PO Box 1051, Springwood QLD, Brisbane, Australia 4127 Tel: 61-7-3-841-2286, Facsimile: 61-7-3-841-2618 ATTN: Messrs. Gordon

Philippines: National Book Store, Inc., Quad Alpha Centrum Bldg, 125 Pioneer Street, Mandaluyong, Metro Manila, Philippines Tel: 632-631-8051, Facsimile: 632-631-5016

Singapore, Malaysia, Brunei, Indonesia: Times Book Shops. Direct sales HQ: STP Distributors, Pasir Panjang Distrientre, Block 1 #03-01A, Pasir Panjang Rd, Singapore 118480 Tel: 65-2767626, Facsimile: 65-2767119

Japan: Phoenix Associates Co., Ltd., Mizuho Bldng, 3-F, 2-12-2, Kami Osaki, Shinagawa-Ku, Tokyo 141 Tel: 81-33-443-7231, Facsimile: 81-33-443-7640 ATTN: Mr. Peter Owans

CANADA

Crisp Learning Canada, 60 Briarwood Avenue, Mississauga, ON L5G 3N6 Canada Tel: 905-274-5678, Facsimile: 905-278-2801 ATTN: Mr. Steve Connolly/Mr. Jerry McNabb

Trade Book Stores: Raincoast Books, 8680 Cambie Street, Vancouver, BC V6P 6M9 Canada Tel: 604-323-7100, Facsimile: 604-323-2600 ATTN: Order Desk

EUROPEAN UNION

England: Flex Training, Ltd., 9-15 Hitchin Street, Baldock, Hertfordshire, SG7 6A, England Tel: 44-1-46-289-6000, Facsimile: 44-1-46-289-2417 ATTN: Mr. David Willetts

INDIA

Multi-Media HRD, Pvt., Ltd., National House, Tulloch Road, Appolo Bunder, Bombay, India 400-039 Tel: 91-22-204-2281, Facsimile: 91-22-283-6478 ATTN: Messrs. Aggarwal

SOUTH AMERICA

Mexico: Grupo Editorial Iberoamerica, Nebraska 199, Col. Napoles, 03810 Mexico, D.F. Tel: 525-523-0994, Facsimile: 525-543-1173 ATTN: Señor Nicholas Grepe

SOUTH AFRICA

Alternative Books, PO Box 1345, Ferndale 2160, South Africa Tel: 27-11-792-7730, Facsimile: 27-11-792-7787 ATTN: Mr. Vernon de Haas